12.95

OLDER EMPLOYEES:

NEW ROLES
FOR
VALUED RESOURCES

OLDER EMPLOYEES:
NEW ROLES FOR VALUED RESOURCES

by Benson Rosen
and
Thomas H. Jerdee

DOW JONES-IRWIN
Homewood, Illinois 60430

© DOW JONES-IRWIN, 1985

This publication is designed to provide accurate and
authoritative information in regard to the subject matter
covered. It is sold with the understanding that the
publisher is not engaged in rendering legal, accounting, or
other professional service. If legal advice or other expert
assistance is required, the services of a competent
professional person should be sought.

*From a Declaration of Principles jointly adopted by a Committee
of the American Bar Association and a Committee of Publishers.*

ISBN 0-87094-439-8

Library of Congress Catalog Card No. 83-73720

Printed in the United States of America

1 2 3 4 5 6 7 8 9 0 ML 2 1 0 9 8 7 6 5

*To the many managers and others who are working to provide
opportunities, support, and encouragement for older employees;
and
to Dusty and Kek in their golden years.*

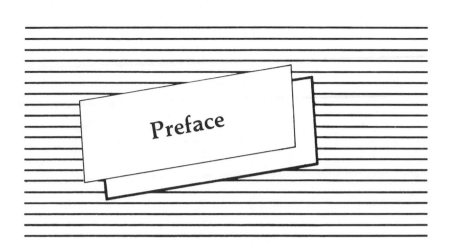

Preface

The goal of this book is to contribute to effective management of older employees. Effective management in this context means helping each older employee to realize his or her full potential for productive and remunerative work activity in keeping with personal desires. It includes planning and phasing into a happy retirement.

Many older employees feel that they have contributed their fair share and more to their organizations and to society, and they may be interested in realizing dreams of tapering off at work in order to take up other activities. We believe that they should be given this opportunity, commensurate with personal, organizational, and societal economic realities. We believe that employers have an obligation to work with them in saving and planning for retirement on a schedule that best fits their needs and capabilities.

Many other older employees find their greatest continuing joys at the workplace. Rather than thinking of retirement, they may be thinking of new challenges, new learning, new ways to serve at work. We believe that they too should be provided with opportunities to realize their dreams.

Perhaps most older employees fall somewhere between these two positions, harboring ambivalent feelings in regard to work and retirement. They too need help to develop career and retirement strategies that best serve their long-run interests. They should be given this help.

The needs of older employees are in themselves a powerful cause for management concern, but in addition there are the very real needs of organizations for the stability, wisdom, and know-how represented among older employees. These latter needs are likely to become much more visible in forthcoming decades.

We believe that the vast majority of managers want to enrich the lives of older employees and draw on their strengths. We also believe that we have something new and special to say to these managers. Through a series of research studies, we have examined a variety of phenomena relating to the older employee. In this book, we draw on these studies to address a number of important issues. We integrate our findings with those of others, as a basis for raising challenges, suggesting policies and procedures, and offering encouragement to managers who want to help the older employee.

We have included a large number of cases and incidents throughout the book. Some of these illustrate the day-to-day problems and career barriers encountered by older workers. Others show how enlightened human resource policies implemented by many companies contribute to the fair and equitable treatment of senior employees. Still others highlight the kinds of interpersonal skills that managers can develop to work effectively with their older colleagues. The cases and incidents dramatize the good faith efforts of many individuals to create the kinds of organizational climates that promote and support the full and productive contributions of all workers.

We also provide practical insights and suggestions, drawn from the professional literature on human resource management and from the experience of dozens of organizations.

Our work on management of older employees has benefited greatly from the support of the Administration on Aging, the University of North Carolina Business Foundation, and countless participants in our research efforts. We are also indebted to the many other researchers working in the field of aging and employment.

Some critics argue that America's return on investments in aging research and advocacy is woefully inadequate.[1] While we agree that much more needs to be done to help the elderly, we are impressed by the progress manifested in the pages of the National Council on the Aging's journal, *Aging and Work,* and in the many other sources drawn on in this book.

We hope and trust that you who read this book will find it helpful in carrying forward and bringing to fruition the efforts of so many others on behalf of the elderly worker.

Benson Rosen
Thomas H. Jerdee

---

[1]Carroll L. Estes, *The Aging Enterprise* (San Francisco: Jossey-Bass, 1979).

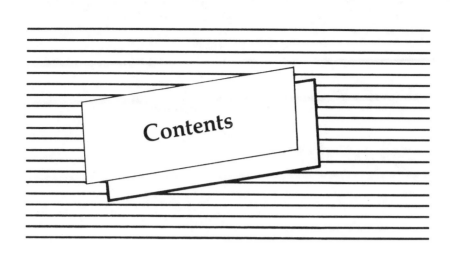

Contents

1.	The Challenge of Managing Older Employees	2
2.	The Age Stereotyping Process	14
3.	How Age Stereotypes Influence Managerial Decisions	34
4.	Age Discrimination Law	52
5.	Career Planning and Management for Older Employees	82
6.	Assessing Performance, Potential, and Health	108
7.	Combating Obsolescence	126
8.	Flexible Retirement Systems	140
9.	Working with Senior Employees	164
10.	Putting It All Together: Organizational Strategies	182
11.	Guidelines for Change	192
	Index of Cases by Topic	195
	Index	197

OLDER
EMPLOYEES:

NEW ROLES
FOR
VALUED RESOURCES

The Challenge of Managing Older Employees

Main Issues

- Economic pressures to delay retirement are mounting.
- Preventing employee obsolescence in the face of rapid technological change is a growing challenge to management.

- Legal protections for older workers require positive steps from management.
- A major push for extending work lives will soon be under way.

The aim of this book is to provide readers with concepts and strategies for effective management of older employees. Fair and helpful treatment of older employees should be a high-priority management goal at any time, but it is especially deserving of attention right now. The requirements for effective management of older employees are changing rapidly. A challenge of major proportions is developing out of current technological, economic, and legal changes.

To meet this new challenge, managers must have more than a desire to help the older employee. They must have an appreciation of the strengths, weaknesses, and special needs of older employees. They must have a knowledge of the special legal requirements that apply to older employees. Most importantly, they must know how to develop and implement specific action plans aimed at helping older employees work up to their full potential in a changing work environment. This requires not only a desire to help but also the specific knowledge presented in this book. Before turning to that knowledge, let us examine in greater detail the nature of the current challenge.

Nature of the Challenge

Treatises on the older employee often begin with tales of century-old grocery clerks, octogenarian executives, and chorus girls in their sexy 60s, all

of whom are cited as proof that if managers would only drop their prejudices and offer a little help and encouragement to older employees, all
would be well. If only the challenge of managing older employees were
that simple!

The truth is that few managers harbor prejudice against the older employee. In fact, most managers would be pleased to have employees with
the drive, verve, and wit of octogenarian Congressman Claude Pepper.
Furthermore, when faced directly with the plight of an older employee
who is having difficulty, the vast majority of managers will go out of their
way to extend a helping hand.

Problems arise for managers, however, when they are faced with more
far-reaching personnel decisions affecting the careers of older employees.
Decisions on matters such as promotion, demotion, transfer, job assignments, training, compensation, and personal leave are especially difficult
when the prospect of age-related physical or mental decline is lurking in
the background. Add to this the possibility of an age discrimination suit,
and you have a challenging situation.

Take the case of Paul Stanley. Paul is district sales manager for Apex
Supply Company. He has been with the company for 27 years and has just
celebrated his 63d birthday. Paul is proud of his performance as a sales
manager. His hard work building customer loyalty has paid off with the
highest rate of repeat sales in the company. Lately, however, he has had
some rough going. Several of his best accounts have either gone out of
business or sold out to companies that are under long-term contract with
other suppliers. More ominous from Apex's point of view is Paul's weak
record for new account generation in recent years. Paul himself is aware
that he has been spending too much time on maintaining his old standby
accounts and not enough time on cultivating new accounts. When Paul
does go out after new accounts, the reception seems chilly, especially
when he runs into young computer whizzes who start asking questions
about systems compatibility.

Paul's manager is now considering whether it is time to have a long talk
with Paul, a Willy Loman "Death of a Salesman" talk. Or would it be better just to let things rock along awhile longer? If no action is taken and
Paul's sales continue to deteriorate, what will that do to Apex's profitabil-
ity and Paul's self-esteem? Another strategy might be to find another job
for Paul, but what job, and how would Paul react to the change? Paul's
manager finds himself returning to the idea of encouraging Paul to retire,
but he knows that Paul would find this hard to accept. Maybe the best
thing to do is to ride it out and wait for Paul's retirement at age 65. But
suppose Paul decides to keep on working beyond age 65. Doesn't the law
now protect him until age 70?

Until recently, few managers have been overburdened with difficult decisions involving older employees like Paul Stanley. The normal pattern

has been for most employees to maintain their productivity at a satisfactory level until they reach retirement at 65, or in many cases earlier. In the instances where management has had concerns about the falling productivity of older employees, those concerns have been tempered by the certainty of imminent retirement. Now, however, most employees can continue to work until at least age 70 if they so desire.

Recently, we interviewed several personnel officers from large organizations in order to get their perceptions of the challenge posed by the new retirement law. It appeared that we had zeroed in on a great nonissue. Although the managers with whom we talked were still adjusting to ERISA and the Age Discrimination in Employment Act Amendments of 1978, they showed no signs of fear and trembling at the mention of older employees. The reason for their unconcern was that a very small percentage of their employees were approaching the traditional retirement age, and virtually all of these employees were planning to retire "on time" or early. There simply was very little reason to be concerned about the retirement issue. Furthermore, the prospect of age discrimination suits from employees still in their 40s and 50s seemed very remote. Most of the latter group were seen as quite well settled and satisfied.

Currently, however, several trends are converging to produce a much greater challenge for managers of older employees. Three trends stand out:

1. The nature of work is changing in ways that affect older employees in particular.
2. Economic pressures to delay retirement are mounting.
3. Legal protections for older employees are being extended.

In the remainder of this chapter, we examine how each of these three trends affects the management of older employees. In later chapters, we recommend actions for management. Considered in their entirety, the actions we propose are quite sweeping. Implementation, however, can proceed one step at a time to suit the special circumstances of each organization.

Effects of the Changing Nature of Work

In what ways has your own work changed in the past few years? The odds are quite good that you have experienced one or more of the following changes:

1. Your organization's products or services have changed, requiring you to deal with new kinds of information, people, and machines.
2. You have had to learn how to deal with computers and their outputs.

3. The structure of your organization has changed so that your own responsibilities and authority have changed.
4. Your job has been eliminated. You have been laid off. You have switched jobs or even careers, gone back to school, or retired.

If you have not personally experienced one or more of these changes in recent years, they are no doubt familiar to you through the experiences of relatives, friends, or co-workers. Changes in the nature of work have touched the lives of almost all American workers. Rapid change will continue and will have increasingly important implications for the management of older employees. Let us take a closer look at how jobs are changing and at how this affects older workers in particular.

One important change that benefits the older employee is virtually complete. This is the reduction in the physical demands of work, which has been a major goal of humankind through the ages. Thousands of years ago, humans discovered ways to reduce the most arduous physical labor through the use of simple mechanical devices such as the sled, the lever, and the wheel. Humans also learned that the energy to operate these devices could be supplied by domesticated animals, and later by mechanical power plants. During the industrial revolution, the role of gross human muscle power was reduced dramatically. In present-day America, only a very small fraction of human work makes heavy demands on muscle power. This has been good for the older employee because the decline in muscular strength that accompanies aging is seldom consequential at work.

Instead of supplying muscle power, millions of workers have been employed in roles that are less demanding physically. They have been serving as operators of their mechanical creations. Much work, whether in the factory or in the office, has involved the guidance and control of machines. Although the work itself may have been routine, repetitive, and unexciting, the pay and fringe benefits have been good, and worker fears of obsolescence have been minimal because changes in machinery and methods have come gradually. In most respects, the work environment has been reasonably beneficent for older employees. Managers have had little reason to be especially concerned about the fate of older employees.

Currently, however, this picture is changing rapidly as a result of the electronic revolution. Electronic devices are replacing humans as monitors and controllers of complex machinery. Manufacturing operations are being robotized so as to eliminate routine operative jobs. Some experts predict that factory jobs may account for less than 10 percent of employment by the turn of the century. For example, a Japanese robot manufacturing plant built in 1981 is depicted as follows in Bruce Nussbaum's *The World after Oil*:

> There is very little light in this factory. There is none of the fluorescent glare
> so typical of plant floors. The entire area, two football fields in size, just

glows dimly. Something else is also different here. The air-conditioning is turned way down, and the air is stale, full of metallic smells. . . . There are no people here—none at all. No voices, no sneezing, no coughing, no laughing. Just the sound of machines.[1]

Clerical and communications operations are undergoing analogous changes. There seems to be no end to the kinds of operations that can be performed effectively by computerized technology. As a result, the demand for workers in the old middle-range skilled and semiskilled operative and clerical occupations is dwindling. True, new jobs are being created in fields such as computerization, robotization, and human services, but these jobs require radically new skills. Although the resulting changes in the world of work affect people of all ages, they affect older employees in particular. Let us look at the picture seen by many older employees.

1. They see technological change as a threat to their jobs.
2. They fear or reject the possibility of retraining that involves learning entirely new skills. Such retraining is not an appetizing prospect when one is uncertain of success and when the payback period is curtailed by a policy of mandatory retirement at 70 or an unwritten policy of even earlier retirement.
3. They do not see unions as a source of help because unions are going along with management to eliminate the old jobs and retrain for the new jobs.
4. They do not see government as a source of help because government programs are now being geared toward retraining the most adaptable rather than saving the jobs of the computer-shy.

The preceding picture is particularly prevalent among older employees with limited education and skills. These are often the very people who have a great need to continue working for financial reasons. Their predicament presents a great challenge to managers who care about elderly employees.

Many other older employees see a much rosier picture, one that might easily include many more years of productive employment, but they want a few minor adjustments to be made in their work situation. These are people who have the necessary background and skills to cope with the electronic revolution. They are not intimidated by the prospect of continuing education and training. In fact, they thrive on continuing challenge and are eager to participate in new technologies. For various reasons, however, they may desire to work a little bit less, to be freed from the straitjacket of the 5-day, 40-hour week or the arduous commute to the workplace. To put the matter more generally, they may wish to be liberated from the controls on time and place of work implied by traditional employment contracts. They may want more flexibility and discretion in

---

[1]Bruce Nussbaum, *The World after Oil* (New York: Simon & Schuster, 1983), pp. 19–20.

their work. Many may want to work at home on a full- or part-time basis, perhaps for more than one employer. Others may be especially attracted by the prospect of a work station away from home, but not far away, so that they can gain the benefit of getting out and being with other people without the hassles of a difficult commute. Thus another challenge for managers is to develop arrangements for time and place of work that will enable these talented older employees to continue in productive employment.

In summary, current changes in the nature of work are threatening to older employees with limited skills but challenging and intriguing to other, more adaptable older employees. Of course, the preceding dichotomization of older employees into haves and have-nots is somewhat artificial. Large numbers of older employees are likely to be somewhere between the two extremes, hopeful but somewhat uncertain about their future work life. Management's challenge is to find ways to help all employees maintain their employability and to offer working arrangements that will appeal to those managerially or technologically talented older employees who might otherwise choose to retire.

Effects of Economic Pressures to Delay Retirement

Until recent times, people worked until they were no longer able to do so or until they had amassed sufficient savings to enable them to retire. The decision to retire was based on health and wealth, not on age. With the advent of social security and various government and private pension plans, large numbers of people began aiming for retirement at age 65 or earlier. This trend has continued right up to the present. Many government employees retire in their 50s, after 30 years of service. Similar patterns have taken hold in industries with labor contracts favoring early retirement.

Now, however, we are beginning to see the economic wisdom of reversing this trend toward early retirement. Even for those favored employees who can count on government pensions or on social security supplemented by private pensions or savings, there frequently is no assurance that retirement income will be an adequate shield against the ravages of inflation. As a result, many older employees are strongly interested in finding ways to sustain their real income. Some may even be desperate to keep on working for financial reasons. So a good deal of economic pressure for delayed retirement is generated within the elderly employee group, sometimes out of dire necessity.

Pressures for later retirement are also being exerted by economists, government officials, and industrial leaders who are concerned about the costs to society of maintaining a large proportion of the population in

Age of Population

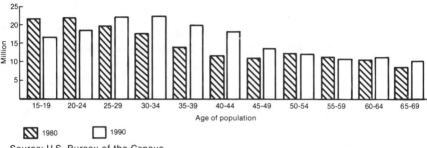

Source: U.S. Bureau of the Census.

forced idleness. Such pressures have been most clearly manifested in recent changes in social security regulations. The eligibility age for full benefits will gradually be raised to 67 by the year 2027. Early retirement benefits at age 62, currently 80 percent, will be reduced to 70 percent. The earnings penalty taken out of social security benefits for retired workers earning over $6,600 per year will be reduced in 1990 to 33 percent, from the current 50 percent.

Counteracting the pressures for delaying retirement are pressures from younger employees to "clear out the deadwood" or "make room on the ladder." Managers often find themselves caught in the middle between these opposing points of view. Delaying retirement should win out because it makes sense from the basic economic standpoint of getting more people to contribute to the stream of goods and services that are available for consumption. Others argue further that in the coming two decades changing population demographics will produce worker shortages that can be met only by delaying the retirement of older employees. These shortages, however, may be confined to the talented elite among senior employees, those with highly valued experience and know-how. For many other older employees, the only shortage may be a shortage of cash that can be remedied only by delaying retirement, if their employers will enable them to do so.

In summary, many individual older employees are being pushed by economic realities in the direction of delayed retirement. Macroeconomic forces are likewise signaling the need to keep more older people working longer. Managers are challenged to find ways to make this possible and profitable without detriment to the short-run interests of younger workers.

Effects of Legal Pressures

In a recent comprehensive review of legal trends affecting employment relations, Gerson and Britt stated that "the major focal point in the employment discrimination area will shift to age discrimination."[2]

Indeed, legal pressures are already contributing greatly to the challenge of managing older employees. Two laws stand out, the Age Discrimination in Employment Act as amended in 1978 and the Employee Retirement Income Stabilization Act of 1974. The latter act governs technical aspects of pension programs and is therefore of great concern to pension specialists but a bit beyond the scope of our discussion here. We shall focus instead on the challenge posed by the Age Discrimination in Employment Act, which has broad implications for every older employee and for all managers. In a later chapter, we shall deal with the specifics of the act. At this point, we shall examine briefly the nature of the challenge generated by the act.

The Age Discrimination in Employment Act provides specific protection against discrimination in employment decisions for employees and job applicants between the ages of 40 and 70. This means that managers must be scrupulously fair to employees in this age range and must also build the documentation necessary to protect the organization from age discrimination litigation. What does being fair entail? It means that job assignments, training opportunities, promotions, pay increases, and all other personnel decisions must be made without regard to employee age. Even decisions about retirement are covered by the act until age 70. It has taken many employees (and we dare say employers as well) some time to become acquainted with the scope of the act's coverage. In particular, there is confusion about the minimum age for forced retirement, which is now 70. Because social security is geared to age 65, many people think that companies can require retirement at age 65. This, however, is not the case, and people are beginning to find this out. In view of their economic need for continued income, more people are becoming interested in working beyond age 65. Managers must find ways to accommodate these people and also to assure their fair treatment with regard to opportunities for training and development.

The frequency of costly age discrimination suits has been increasing. Furthermore, the reach of the law is likely to be extended to include a requirement that government contractors establish affirmative action programs not only for minorities and females, but also for older workers, covering both full-time and part-time work. All of this means that managers must work hard at developing their older employees, maintaining their effectiveness, keeping them happy, and documenting any actions

---

[2]Herbert E. Gerson and Louis P. Britt III, "Legal Trends," *Personnel Administrator* 28, no. 12 (December 1983), p. 18.

that might be viewed as adverse to the interests of any older employee or job candidate. Managers must also guard against charges of reverse discrimination from younger employees.

Although abiding by the letter of age discrimination law is sometimes difficult, abiding by its spirit should be a welcome challenge for most managers. For the most part, the law requires actions that managers are going to take regardless of the law. Problems arise, however, in situations where older employees are having difficulty in coping with work demands or in responding to training opportunities. When an older employee is having difficulty in keeping up on the job but documentation is difficult, the manager is in a tough position. Situations like the Paul Stanley case described earlier in this chapter are becoming more common and more difficult for management because many older employees are feeling increased economic and social pressure to continue working and are also becoming more aware of their legal protections.

In summary, managers are challenged by the law to treat all employees, regardless of age, as fairly as possible. This is something that they want to do anyway, but the law challenges them to do it just a little better and to keep much better documentation of their efforts.

What Managers Must Do

In this chapter, we have discussed challenges for the management of older employees that arise out of the changing nature of work, the changing economic environment, and the changing legal environment. To a very great extent, these challenges boil down to finding better ways to develop and utilize the skills of older employees and to avoid wasteful premature retirement. These are goals that are readily acceptable to the vast majority of American managers. What, specifically, needs to be done by individual managers in order to achieve them? Let us look at a few suggestions that might be helpful in converting the general challenge into more specific challenges that individual managers can address with action.

1. Managers are challenged to examine their own perceptions about the capabilities and appropriate roles of older employees. The issue here is not ill will or bias but possible misinformation or error. This challenge is addressed in detail in Chapters 2 and 3, on age stereotypes and their effects on managerial actions.
2. Managers are challenged to be thoroughly familiar with laws affecting the management of older employees. This challenge is addressed in detail in Chapter 4.
3. Managers are challenged to develop and implement comprehensive systems of career management for older employees. This challenge is addressed in Chapter 5.

4. Managers are challenged to develop and implement accurate and fair systems for assessing the performance and potential of older employees. This challenge is addressed in Chapter 6.
5. Managers are challenged to develop and implement effective systems for maintaining and improving the work skills of older employees. This challenge is addressed in Chapter 7.
6. Managers are challenged to develop and implement flexible retirement systems that maximize opportunities for continued work contributions within the capabilities and desires of older employees. This challenge is addressed in Chapter 8.
7. Managers are challenged to work at the interpersonal level to help each individual older employee achieve optimal work adjustment and a smooth transition to retirement. This challenge is addressed in Chapter 9.
8. Managers are challenged to integrate all of these activities into coherent organizational programs that will be a source of benefit and pride to themselves, to their organizations, and to all Americans. This is discussed in Chapter 10.

This may appear to be a rather full agenda, and in truth it is. Keep in mind, however, that all of these challenges need not be addressed simultaneously. It is up to each manager to determine what actions deserve highest priority in his or her special organizational situation.

A Final Point: The Long-Term Imperative

The challenge facing managers in the near term will not be caused by a flood of older workers demanding their rights. In the next few years, we are more likely to see a shortage of seasoned older employees rather than a difficult-to-manage surplus. However, the age distribution of our population is such that we will be faced with a dramatic change in about the year 2010, when large numbers of post–World War II "baby boomers," born around 1950, will be reaching traditional retirement ages. Who will produce the goods and services for them to consume? With the low birthrates of the 1960s through the present, there will be too few people in the traditional working ages to carry all the oldsters. When that happens, it will be critically important for the economy as a whole and for individual organizations to extend the work lives of the baby boomers. Organizations that have developed flexible and positive policies and practices for the management of older employees will have a clear edge. Forward-looking organizations should begin action now. Regardless of these important long-term considerations, individual managers will want to act now because it is right to do so.

2

The Age Stereotyping Process

Main Issues

- Age stereotypes are pervasive in our culture.

- Stereotypes depicting older employees as lower in performance capacity and potential for development are largely unfounded.

- Stereotypes depicting older employees as stable and interpersonally competent are accurate.

- Stereotypes of declining physical capacity are partially correct. Physical capacity and health should be monitored on an individual basis.

- Most of the elderly have considerable potential for continued productive participation in our society, and their participation is needed.

Carl Adams wondered how the new territory manager would affect the already tarnished sales performance of his Midwest region. Last year the region fell far below budget. Personnel problems were largely responsible for the poor performance. During the past year, Carl had trained one territory manager, only to lose him to a competitor. Last month he fired another territory manager for consistently poor sales performance. It seemed to Carl that in recent years some of the old-timers had lost the aggressiveness needed to land big accounts and new recruits often lacked the technical knowledge needed to sell the company's most profitable systems. Carl knew that for his region to make budget, the newly hired territory manager would have to hit the ground running.

New territory managers were recruited through the company's corporate headquarters in Chicago, so Carl had little control over the selection process. However, the regional manager was permitted to send back or veto a referral from headquarters, with written justification. Sifting through the new recruit's résumé, Carl noted that the year of high school graduation was listed as 1945, almost five years before Carl was born. A rough calculation led Carl to estimate his new employee's age to be around 57 or 58.

Carl and the other regional sales managers had often discussed the qualities necessary for a successful career in sales. Excellent planning and time management skills, product knowledge, and superb interpersonal abilities ranked at the top of their list. The regional sales managers agreed that the territory sales position required an individual who was not afraid to make contact with new prospects—what the regional managers referred to as a willingness to slam the car door 8 or 10 times a day.

Would a 57-year-old salesman have the energy, aggressiveness, and perseverance necessary to manage a highly competitive territory? Could a 57-year-old recruit demonstrate the versatility and future orientation required to keep pace with the rapid changes in products and equipment that the company planned to introduce in the coming years? Would an older employee respond well to guidance and motivational efforts coming from a supervisor young enough to be his son?

Carl Adams had never vetoed a referral from headquarters. However, he had never before been faced with the prospect of two consecutive below-budget years in the Midwest region.

The Nature of Age Stereotypes

Put yourself in Carl Adams' place for a moment. You are a 33-year-old regional sales manager who learns that a 57-year-old man has been recruited to work under your supervision. What are your expectations about the likelihood that your new employee will succeed? About how well he will take direction and respond to your coaching? About whether you can count on him to stay current with your changing lines of products and technological hardware?

In the absence of any further information about the 57-year-old rookie territory manager, your answers to these questions will be influenced, at least in part, by your expectations about the capacities and motivations of a typical 57-year-old person. In other words, your stereotypes about people in the 55–60 age category influenced how you reacted in this case. Some readers probably viewed the appointment of the older territory manager as providing the maturity and experience necessary to turn around the Midwest region's sales slump. Other readers probably saw the 57-year-old rookie as a poor bet to show the dedication needed to stay current with a rapidly changing product line and the drive needed to succeed in sales.

In this chapter, we will take a close look at the development of stereotypes, at commonly held age stereotypes, and at the validity of age stereotypes for predicting the attitudes and behaviors of older workers. Since we often unconsciously decide how to interact with others based on expectations about how they are likely to respond, it is particularly important to examine the accuracy of our assumptions. Erroneous assumptions can give rise to complex self-fulfilling prophecies that bring out the worst in others and confirm our expectations for all of the wrong reasons.

Stereotyping is making judgments about others on the basis of their membership in a particular group. Once group membership has been established, assigning to specific individuals traits or characteristics thought to be descriptive of most or all members of the group is almost a reflexive response. Typical stereotypes are based on age, sex, or membership in racial, ethnic, or occupational groups.

Examples of stereotyping are the assumption that all Englishmen are good sports, that all Japanese workers are concerned with quality and productivity, and that all professors are absentminded and out of touch with the real world. While such stereotypes represent a handy shortcut for forming impressions and making decisions, in many instances the attributes associated with a group do not apply to all of its members. Stereotypes fail to account for individual differences among members within a particular category.

In a business context, decisions based on race, sex, or age stereotypes run the risk of ignoring or misjudging individual differences in talents, capabilities, and motivations. Accordingly, business decisions based on stereotypical assumptions about various categories of employees can prove both erroneous and costly, impairing self-esteem, impeding career progress, and resulting in an underutilization of human resources. Moreover, stereotyping may lead to illegal differential treatment of particular employee groups.

Since the focus in this book is on older employees, we will examine job-related age stereotypes. Examining how managers make judgments about the likely performance and potential of older workers should give valuable insights into the areas where older workers are viewed as particularly effective or particularly limited.

Think about the numerous clichés that are commonly used to describe older workers and organizational responses to the problems surrounding work and retirement. Expressions such as the following have become part of our everyday vocabulary:

You can't teach an old dog new tricks.

Over the hill.

Marking time.

Fading fast.

Frail and fragile.

On the shelf.

Out to pasture.

Ready for the scrap heap.

Ready for the gold watch.

The old man, pops, dad, old fogy, geezer.

One foot in the grave.

Slightly senile.

Old as the hills.

She drives like a little old lady from Pasadena.

Not all of the clichés used in connection with older workers are negative, however, as illustrated in the following examples:

The wisdom of age.

Loyal to the end.

Not older, but better.

Aging like fine wine.

Never too old to learn.

Origins of Age Stereotypes

Stereotypes are learned ways of organizing and perceiving the world. The content of stereotypes is affected by cultural factors, social and economic variables, family and peer pressures, and our own firsthand observations. For example, cultural differences account for the way older people are viewed and treated in different countries. In Japan older people are treated with great respect and deference, and in Sweden government provisions designed to maintain the independence and dignity of senior citizens have long been the rule. By contrast, in recent years the United States has been very youth oriented. The fashion and cosmetics industries thrive on creating a young look. Perhaps the most extreme view is taken by primitive tribes that regard the elderly as a drain on scarce resources and expect them to wander off and die quietly so that they will not become a burden on other tribesmen.

Interestingly, direct contact with a group is not a prerequisite for developing stereotypes about it. For many years, schoolchildren's perceptions of American Indians were shaped by one-dimensional textbook descriptions and cowboy movies. Similarly, researchers in the 1950s discovered that some schoolchildren in the South held well-developed stereotypes of blacks, even though many had never actually encountered black people.

Of course, most stereotypes are based on firsthand experience. Consider the contrast between the attitudes of David and Donald. David, age eight, thoroughly enjoys Saturday morning fishing trips with his grandfather. Young David appreciates his grandfather's knowledge of the outdoors, enthusiasm and good humor, and patience as a teacher and friend. Based on this positive experience, David views the elderly as wise, fun-loving, and "neat."

Donald, also age eight, lives next door to an elderly man who is easily annoyed by loud kids and barking dogs. He frequently expresses his distaste for both to anyone who passes through the neighborhood. Donald develops a perception of older persons as cranky complainers, or as he puts it, "Old guys are public enemies of kids."

Comparing the experiences of David and Donald helps clarify how differences in expectations about older persons develop from early childhood. Often parents reinforce these expectations. In one family the visit of an elderly relative is eagerly anticipated as a joyous event, while in another family Aunt Sara's visits are dreaded like the plague. Depiction of the elderly on television, on the radio, and in newspapers as weak, ugly, ill-tempered, and inept further shapes expectations and stereotypes.

In a business context, one-of-a kind experiences with older workers can similarly shape perceptions, particularly when we have been predisposed to think of older persons in certain ways because of past experiences. When a production manager encounters an older employee who frequently misses work due to illness, he may come to view all older workers as chronic absentees. Similarly, an account executive who supervises a very conservative older investment adviser may come to view all older employees as risk averse.

Job-Related Age Stereotypes

In order to understand just how older people are viewed, we recently conducted a systematic investigation. A 65-item age stereotype questionnaire was developed. The items were derived from three sources: (1) scientific writings regarding physical and psychological differences between various age groups, (2) depictions of older people in the popular media, and (3) attributes judged important for effective organizational performance.

On the basis of content, the 65 items were classified into four work-related scales: performance capacity (productive, creative, efficient), potential for development (capable of learning, versatile, eager to achieve), stability (careful, dependable, steady), and interpersonal skills (aware of others' feelings and effective in group situations).

Groups of businesspeople and university business students were asked to participate in a study designed to learn more about job-related age stereotypes. Each participant was instructed to imagine that he would soon meet two people for the first time and that the only information available was that one of them would be a 60-year-old man and that the other would be a 30-year-old man. The participants were asked to consider the list of 65 characteristics and indicate the degree to which each characteristic described the average 60-year-old male and the average 30-year-old male. Raters indicated the degree to which they judged each characteristic to be descriptive of an older or younger person on a 10-point scale anchored by 0, "not at all accurate," and 9, "very accurate." The instructions stressed that there were no right or wrong answers, and the participants were encouraged to give their own honest and frank opinions.

FIGURE 2-1

Age Stereotypes

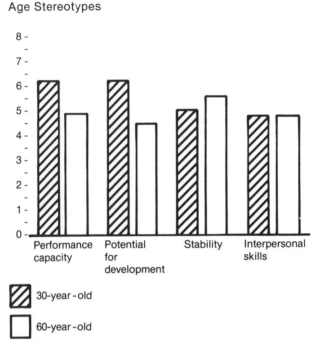

The results are presented in Figure 2–1. Comparisons were made on the mean rating scores on each scale for the 30-year-old man and the 60-year-old man.

Performance Capacity

The items in this scale reflect perceived differences in the way younger and older men respond to job performance demands. The younger man was seen as consistently more productive, efficient, motivated, and capable of working under pressure. The older man was seen as more accident-prone.

Potential for Development

Again, the perceived differences favored the younger man. He was seen not only as more ambitious, eager, and future oriented but also as more receptive to new ideas, more capable of learning, more adaptable, and more versatile. The older man was seen as more rigid and more dogmatic.

Stability

The ratings on this dimension favored the older man. He was seen as more reliable, more honest and trustworthy, and less likely to quit or miss work for personal reasons.

Interpersonal Skills

No consistent differences were found on this scale. The younger man was rated higher on some components of interpersonal skill, and the older man was rated higher on others. It appears that there was no clearly defined stereotype regarding age differences in interpersonal skills.

Effects of Rater's Age

The relationship between the rater's age and the tendency to see differences between younger and older workers was also examined. The only consistent pattern of evaluation differences attributable to the rater's age was on the performance capacity scale. Older participants perceived less difference between the younger and older employee. With this one exception, managers of all ages appear equally likely to see major differences between younger and older employees.

In summary, these research findings suggest the existence of age stereotypes that depict an older person as potentially less employable than a younger person, particularly for highly demanding positions, and as less interested in change and less capable of coping with future challenges. The older man was perceived to be less capable of effective performance with respect to creative, motivational, and productive job demands. The older man was also rated as lower in potential for development.

Returning to the case with which we opened this chapter, it is now easy to understand why regional sales manager Carl Adams may have held some very negative expectations about the likely performance of his newly assigned 57-year-old territory manager. The territory manager's position required many of the characteristics commonly assumed to be lacking in older workers. Moreover, widely held stereotypes depict older workers as unwilling or unable to learn new behaviors and adjust to changing job demands. To the extent that Carl Adams viewed his new territory manager as unlikely to succeed, the 57-year-old entered his job with two strikes against him.

Accuracy of Age Stereotypes

Common sense suggests that stereotypes describe the mythical "average" representative of various age, race, sex, or occupational groups. Since no one individual in the stereotyped group shares all of the traits or characteristics attributed to the group, stereotypical thinking can lead to false impressions, poor judgments, and inappropriate actions. For example, an advertising manager stereotypes his senior copy editor as burned out of creative new ideas and therefore decides to work around the senior copy editor when he launches a major new advertising campaign. If the advertising manager's perception of creative burnout is on target, this decision saves him the time and energy necessary to solicit input from his subordinate. On the other hand, if that perception misses the mark, the advertising manager deprives himself and his colleagues of potentially valuable insights that the senior copy editor might have provided.

A review of the scientific research on work-related differences in the attitudes, performance, and health status of older workers will provide a basis for evaluating the accuracy of age stereotypes.[1] What emerges from this review is a picture of older Americans as a heterogeneous group, including many individuals who show commitment, loyalty, dedication, and good health; and others whose continued organizational contributions may depend on job redesign or job transfer to reduce physical and stress demands, special precautions to reduce accident risks, and training and development to overcome skill obsolescence.

Morale, Commitment, and Involvement

Picture an older worker five years from retirement, and what do you see? For some, the image that comes to mind is one of a senior employee slowly going through the motions of work, totally uninterested in others and uninvolved with them, perhaps brooding about the career that "might have been." Research findings, however, show that images of older workers who mark time while waiting for the traditional gold watch couldn't be farther from the truth.

Overwhelming scientific evidence points to older workers as enjoying higher morale and a greater sense of organizational commitment and job involvement than workers in any other age group. One recent study, involving more than 3,000 workers in a broad range of occupations, found that age was positively associated with ratings of job satisfaction. Older workers tended to rate work as more important to their lives than did other age groups. A review of 20 separate studies confirms the finding that job

---

[1]For a comprehensive review of the scientific literature on the characteristics of older workers, see Mildred Doering, Susan Rhodes, and Michael Schuster, *The Aging Worker: Research and Recommendations*. (Beverly Hills, Calif.: Sage Publications, 1983).

satisfaction tends to increase with age. Perhaps the strongest evidence of this association comes from the report of two University of Michigan researchers who found that workers age 65 and over have the highest job satisfaction of any age group.

Some investigators have attempted to determine what job elements are important to workers in different age categories. Research assessing the job attitudes of almost 2,000 managers found no differences attributable to age on reported desires for fulfilling self-esteem and autonomy needs. Older managers did rate needs for job security as more important than did younger managers. Perhaps the greater financial responsibilities of older managers account for the premium they place on job security. Or perhaps the greater needs of older managers for job security reflect the difficulty that senior managers often encounter in finding positions.

When it comes to satisfaction with pay, no clearly interpretable trend emerges from the research to date. In some studies age was found to be positively related to pay satisfaction, while in other studies age was negatively related to pay satisfaction. Attitudes toward promotion opportunities, supervision, and co-workers showed no clear relationship to employee age. It appears that differences across organizations in personnel policies determine satisfaction with these factors for workers in all age categories.

Involvement with the job depends to a large extent on the nature of the work activities. Research evidence suggests that, compared to their younger counterparts, older workers express greater job involvement across a broad spectrum of organizational positions. Similarly, older workers report a greater sense of organizational commitment across a wide range of organizational contexts.

Job involvement and organizational commitment should be reflected in stated intentions to remain in the organization or to quit. Again, research findings indicate that older workers are much less likely than younger workers to report an intention to leave. Turning from intentions to actual behavior, over 25 studies have examined the relationship between age and turnover. A few of these studies suggest that there is no discernible relationship between age and turnover, but most of the studies report that older workers are much less likely than younger workers to leave the organization. These findings, which have far-reaching implications for human resource planning, investments in training and development, career ladders, and retirement policies, will be examined in more detail in later chapters.

Performance on the Job

A recent review of the scientific evidence on the age-performance relationship covering numerous studies conducted over the past 30 years concluded that there is little support for widely held stereotypes of significant drops in performance associated with aging. Research investigating the performance capacity of blue-collar workers, production workers, clerical workers, engineers, and scientists failed to find a significant performance decline related to aging. In fact, several studies suggested that among groups of paraprofessionals and clerical employees, older workers actually outperformed younger workers. And U.S. Department of Labor studies reveal that, in general, age has little effect on manual workers through age 50. Declines in productivity were never found to exceed 10 percent thereafter. In future years, as the number of jobs requiring strenuous physical activity decreases, the diminishing physical capacities of older workers will probably not be a significant barrier to their continued employment.

Excellent interpersonal skills are required for successful performance in many organizational positions. Evidence suggests that changes in emotional stability and sociability are not related to age.

A very common age stereotype depicts the older worker as dogmatically rigid and set in his ways. Research evidence indicates, however, that dogmatic behavior is also unrelated to age. Another widely held belief is that creative ability declines dramatically with age. Studies of creative scholars and artists suggest the opposite, namely, that creativity generally increases with age.

Age stereotypes frequently depict declines in managerial abilities, including indecisiveness, inability to stay on top of key issues, and loss of good business judgment. Recent research goes a long way toward dispelling these myths. A study involving 1,700 managers working in 10 diverse organizations showed that when managerial performance was measured in terms of such bottom line indicators as return on total capital, growth of stockholders' equity, earnings per share, and sales growth, no significant differences in performance could be related to the age of managers.

Several studies have demonstrated age-related declines in specific abilities or functions. In one study, age differences in intellectual performance reached statistical significance, but these differences were so small that experts concluded that they had virtually no social consequences. Moreover, when intellectual tests stress accuracy rather than speed, many intellectual functions, including numerical abilities and verbal comprehension, are unaffected by age.

Gerontologists have detected age-related declines in speed and accuracy of movement, perception, hearing, vision, and certain types of problem-solving skills. Again, the researchers have concluded that these declines would affect performance in only a few jobs requiring extremely high levels of sensory or cognitive skills.

Finally, three studies report isolated examples of performance declines involving printers over age 50, male production workers over age 55, and clerical workers in the footwear industry over age 65.

The question of major importance for managers faced with the need to maintain productivity and meet corporate objectives concerns the degree to which declines in functional abilities related to age, particularly in areas related to problem solving and decision making, affect the performance of older workers. Recognizing wide variation due to individual differences among older employees, one Harvard gerontologist has called for more information to answer this question. Specifically, he identifies a great need for improvement in the techniques of skill measurement, information processing, and job analysis to determine the actual job relevance of these age-related declines. In general, older workers may learn ways to compensate for any physiological and psychological functions that decline with age. Drawing on years of experience and good judgment, workers over age 60 are functionally able to excel in many occupations.

In summary, evidence on the performance of older workers and managers generally indicates that they perform as well as their younger counterparts on almost all criteria. Thus it is not surprising that gerontologists concur that chronological age is a poor indicator of an individual's mental and physical well-being and an inadequate basis for predicting vocational performance. Individual differences within age groups accounts for much more variation in performance than does age. This in no way diminishes the importance of carefully assessing individual capabilities with an eye toward matching them to job requirements.

Health and Well-Being

Age stereotypes depict older people as frail and fragile, as having lost the vitality and energy necessary to make a full-fledged commitment to their careers. How valid are these stereotypes? Again, the answer must begin with a caution, namely, that large differences exist with respect to the health and well-being of individuals in every age category. While some individuals remain remarkably healthy in their 80s, and even in their 90s, others are mentally and physically old at age 40. In the past decade, however, changes in lifestyles, dietary habits, and exercise patterns, along with the introduction of new life-prolonging medical interventions, have dramatically changed the health picture for the elderly.

Life expectancy is increasing, and perhaps more importantly, older people today enjoy much better health than did those living in past generations. Yet there is no denying that major bodily changes occur throughout the life cycle. Here are some of the facts about the effects of aging on physical, sensory, and bodily functions.

Changes in Physical Condition.   As the body ages, bones become lighter and more brittle, vertebrae move closer together, and muscle tone and muscle mass decline. The net effect of these changes is some loss in strength. In addition, lung capacity drops, and the immunity system is more likely to fail as the body ages. Moreover, degenerative diseases, including arthritis, heart disease, and various neurological disorders, are associated with aging. While these diseases can often be controlled with proper medication and are not necessarily obstacles to job performance, the ticking of the biological clock inevitably takes its toll on the human body.

Sensory Declines.   Some losses occur in the senses of vision, hearing, taste, smell, and touch. In many cases, visual and auditory impairments are easily corrected with glasses and hearing aids. For the most part, sensory losses are modest, and sensory activity seldom drops below the threshold levels needed to meet job requirements.

Cognitive Impairments.   Tagging an older person with the label "senile" is perhaps the cruelest and most unjustified stereotype of all. While the deterioration of some mental processes becomes detectable with advancing age, only about 8 percent of the population over age 65 shows indications of significant mental deterioration, such as partial memory loss and a slowing of reaction time. After about age 30, reaction time slows. However, older workers have demonstrated the ability to compensate by increasing their speed on certain complex repetitive tasks.

Changes in cognitive functioning associated with age have profound implications for the design of training and development programs. Since corporate training efforts represent the single most important approach to counteracting technical and managerial obsolescence, it is surprising how little attention has been devoted to developing training technologies tailored to the older student. While much more research should be directed to this issue, preliminary evidence suggests that training approaches that permit self-paced learning and focus on experiential learning rather than abstract learning may be most compatible with the cognitive strengths of older employees.

Functional versus Chronological Age.   An examination of the biological and psychological changes associated with aging accentuates the importance of recognizing differences among individuals in the same age group. In assessments of the continued employability of older workers, the decisive factor should be functional age rather chronological age.

Recently, Leon Koyl, a specialist in industrial medicine, advanced the concept of measuring both individual and position requirements on seven functional dimensions. Koyl's approach, called GULHEMP, begins with an analysis of the levels of physical functioning necessary to perform a job. Prospective employees are given a comprehensive physical examination to determine their functional capacities on each of the seven dimensions. Job assignments are made on the basis of ability to perform the necessary functions above threshold levels.

The measurement of functional ability shifts attention from the employee's functional limitations, what he can't do, to his functional capacities, what he can do. Understanding the capacities and limitations associated with various medical impairments permits managers to judge more accurately the job relevance of various health problems and to avoid overreaction to minor problems that may not interfere with an employee's ability to continue working.

The GULHEMP system and others like it should do much to dispel stereotypes regarding the assumed limitations imposed by health problems. Knowledge about the job-related medical consequences of various health conditions will help managers to strike a balance between providing employment opportunities for individuals who can make significant organizational contributions and protecting the right of older employees with nondisabling medical problems to continue working.[2]

Absenteeism

Closely associated with stereotypes about the failing health of older workers are stereotypes that depict older workers as chronic absentees. Examination of the validity of these stereotypes begins with a distinction between what human resource managers have termed avoidable and unavoidable absences. Avoidable absences are typically voluntary decisions to take a day or two off for personal reasons. Research shows that older workers have a much better attendance record than younger workers with respect to such absences.

Unavoidable absences typically involve time off for sanctioned reasons such as serious illness. Unavoidable absences often last longer than avoidable absences. Research findings suggest that there is a direct relationship between age and unavoidable absences. A number of explanations have been given for the relatively poorer record of older workers with respect to unavoidable absences. One explanation is that older workers who are ill or injured require a longer recovery period. An alternative explanation is that older workers have greater exposure to hazardous working conditions or suffer the cumulative effects of noxious chemicals. In either event, when unavoidable absences occur, the time lost may be greater for older employees than for their younger counterparts.

[2]Leon Koyl, *Employing the Older Worker: Matching the Employee to the Job*, 2d ed. (Washington, D.C.: National Council on Aging, 1974).

Older workers have also been pegged as accident-prone. However, industrial psychologists have shown that in many instances older workers are better risks than younger workers across a variety of jobs even when risk exposure is controlled. Moreover, a study based on over a million workers' compensation claims as reported by the Bureau of Labor Statistics shows that occupational injuries occurred at a lower rate for older workers than for younger workers. While these data are difficult to interpret because of the possibility that older workers may avoid dangerous working conditions, they tend to refute the stereotype that older workers are poor accident risks.

In summary, older workers miss work for avoidable reasons less frequently than do younger workers, but they often require more time off to recover from an accident or illness. The accident records of older workers appear to be better than those of younger workers. It seems reasonable to conclude that the stereotypes depicting older workers as chronic absentees and as accident-prone are not valid.

Other Misconceptions

Almost all of the commonly held stereotypes that we have examined have been shown to be false. But there are other misconceptions about the elderly that have also been refuted. These include misconceptions about their economic condition, about their interest and involvement in society, and about their attitudes toward work and retirement. Such misconceptions often underlie the roles assigned to senior citizens on the job and in daily life. To the extent that these roles are based on invalid assumptions and half-truths, thoughtful reexamination of the facts should lead to new roles for a dramatically undervalued social resource.

Economic Plight.   There is a widely held belief that the elderly are hungry and impoverished. A 1982 Louis Harris Poll found that in every single area of economic life, the elderly were perceived to be in much worse condition than was actually true. While elderly people who must live on fixed-rate pensions and annuities have been hurt by inflation, economists have found that between the years 1970 and 1978 the per capita income of the elderly grew at a slightly higher rate than that of the rest of the population. Increases in the income of the elderly have come from social security payments, returns on investment, and private pension payouts.

Social Involvement.   Results of a 1983 Gallup Poll refute the notion that people over 65 spend their days watching television soap operas and playing shuffleboard but are totally uninvolved with social and political affairs. According to this poll, older people are more likely to be registered voters (83 percent compared to 69 percent for the general population) and to claim that they vote in national elections (57 percent compared to 37 percent for the general population). The poll also showed that older people are more involved in charitable work than other age groups and that they belong to as many voluntary organizations as do other age groups. Finally, older people are more likely than other age groups to be members of a religious group and to attend religious services.

Through their political parties, their religious affiliations, and such special interest organizations as the National Council on Aging, the American Association of Retired Persons, and the Gray Panthers, older people are becoming a more powerful social and political force. The assumption that they are uninterested or uninvolved is a clearly erroneous age stereotype.

Interest in Learning.   Previously cited research suggested that older people are widely viewed as uninterested in learning and perhaps incapable of expanding their skills and knowledge. However, with more than 1.7 million Americans over age 65 enrolled in institutions of higher education, there is clearly no basis for these stereotypes. As noted by Merrell Clark, vice president of the Academy for Educational Development, "People can start over again, renew themselves, take on new challenges in their 50s, 60s, 70s, 80s, and 90s."

Many older people will need advanced training and education to stay abreast of advances in their present occupations or to launch second careers after retirement. In the future, educators will probably recognize still another new role for the elderly—that of eager and motivated students. Perhaps we will even see the emergence of institutions dedicated exclusively to providing a broad range of learning and training opportunities for the elderly.

Desire to Retire.   A popular view is that the older worker is counting the days until retirement. Expressions such as "30 and out" "the silver handshake," "take the pension and run," and "waiting for the gold watch" reflect the widespread belief that older workers are eagerly anticipating their retirement day. It is true that there has been a trend toward early retirement, but there are no grounds for the notion that all older workers wish to retire at the earliest possible moment. More than half of the respondents to a 1979 Louis Harris Poll stated that they intended to continue working beyond age 65. Another Harris Poll found that 76 percent of retirees would like to be working and that 86 percent opposed mandatory retirement at a fixed age. A 1975 Harris Poll found that life satisfaction among 65-year-olds was significantly higher for those who were employed.

It appears, then, that a majority of older workers want to continue working in some capacity and to make a contribution to society. A challenge for organizational human resource planners will be to create new opportunities that capture the desire of older workers to make significant organizational contributions. These opportunities may involve part-time work, job redesign, organizational retraining, new career paths, consultant roles, and other organizational innovations. As the noted gerontologist Carl Swenson stated in a recent article:

> It will be necessary to make it possible for them [older workers] to change from the work of their younger years to work that is more appropriate for them. This will require retraining older people for work that is within their capacity and is rewarding to them as well as of value to other people. An effective system will require counseling to help them choose work that is within their capacities and available, adult educational facilities that are appropriate, and placement services. A whole new profession of vocational guidance, training, and placement for older workers will have to be developed.[3]

Psychological Functions of Age Stereotypes

According to Harold Sheppard, adviser to President Carter on problems of the elderly, "Discrimination against older people is more ingrained in Americans' minds than sexism or racism." Once acquired, age stereotypes shape the way we organize and perceive the world. Deeply ingrained beliefs about older people and about the roles we expect them to assume on the job and in society are very hard to overcome. These beliefs persist even in the face of research evidence that refutes them. One reason why age stereotypes are particularly resistant to change is that they often serve important psychological functions. In fact, they appear to serve different functions for different people. Drawing on examples from the case of the new territory manager that we introduced at the beginning of this chapter, we will illustrate how age stereotypes satisfy key psychological needs.

Instrumental Function

Stereotypes are instrumental to the extent that holding them is associated with attaining rewards and avoiding punishments. Let us assume for a moment that Carl Adams, the regional sales manager depicted in our case, had previously experienced great difficulty in supervising an older territory manager. Specifically, let us assume that Carl was unsuccessful in

---

[3]Carl Swenson, "A Respectable Old Age," *American Psychologist* 38, no. 3 (March 1983), p. 332.

his efforts to train and coach the manager in the company's new consultative selling philosophy and recognized that his inability to influence the sales strategy of this manager would reflect negatively on his own managerial ability. Carl now assumes that most or all older salesmen are dogmatic and resistant to learning new sales techniques. He therefore objects to the assignment of older salesmen to his territory. Incidentally, his unwillingness to work with older salesmen precludes the possibility of a future positive experience with a flexible and accepting older territory manager and thus protects his age stereotype from challenge.

If Carl's aspirations for advancement to vice president of sales were being blocked by a senior executive who intended to continue working until age 70, an older person would again have become associated with negative consequences. Quite understandably, Carl Adams would develop negative age stereotypes based on two career frustrations that he attributed to older persons.

Ego-Defensive Function

In some instances, age stereotypes are held because they provide protection against inner conflicts and insecurities. Some upwardly mobile managers enter into a mentor-protégé relationship with senior executives. The mentor provides informal counseling and guidance and often works behind the scenes to keep his young protégé's career on track. While such relationships frequently prove mutually beneficial, in a few instances the protégé develops a strong dependence on his mentor. In these instances, the protégé may experience anxiety and insecurity over his ability to function independently. Coping with insecurity takes many possible forms, including severing the relationship, projecting feelings of inferiority, accusing the mentor of clinging to the dependency relationship, and branding the mentor as conservative, dependent, and insecure. Often the rejection of an older mentor follows the same course as that taken by a young person to assert his or her independence from a domineering parent. The end result is the development of very negative attitudes toward the elderly, particularly those in positions of authority.

Value-Expressive Function

Age stereotypes may express values imparted in early childhood and reinforced throughout the socialization period. Parental attitudes and values regarding the proper role of the elderly become internalized and form the core of age stereotypes.

Returning to our case again, let us assume that Carl Adams grew up in a home in which his parents cared for a bedridden uncle. The elderly uncle may have been viewed by family members as a financial and psychological burden, restricting the freedom of everyone in the family. Carl particularly remembers the constant admonitions to play quietly so as not to disturb his uncle's rest. Thus Carl's experiences with the elderly became associated with memories of illness, dependence, and constraints on freedom. Perhaps unconsciously, these childhood memories still cloud his view of older people.

Order Function

Stereotypes provide a framework for establishing order and clarity in a complex world. According to Walter Lippmann, who coined the term *stereotype*, our already existing stereotypes "are an ordered, more or less consistent picture of the world, to which our habits, our tastes, our capacities, our comforts, and our hopes have adjusted themselves. They may not be a complete picture of the world, but they are a picture of a possible world to which we are adapted."[4]

In ambiguous situations, we often revert to stereotypes to provide meaning and reduce uncertainty. Anticipating a meeting with a 57-year-old new employee creates a feeling of uncertainty in the regional manager. What kinds of management problems will the 57-year-old pose for him? In the absence of concrete information, the regional manager falls back on age stereotypes to reduce his uncertainties.

Age stereotypes help simplify and order our perceptual world. They influence the judgments we reach and the actions we take to protect ourselves from anticipated negative consequences; they shield us from our own insecurities; they provide an outlet for the expression of deeply ingrained values; and they reduce uncertainty in ambiguous situations. Understandably, stereotypes that serve these psychological functions are hard to shed.

Summary

Age stereotyping is the process of making judgments about others on the basis of their age. The content of age stereotypes is influenced by cultural and societal factors, family and peers, depictions in the media, and personal experiences.

Age stereotypes are widely held. In an employment context, older workers are often viewed as lacking the motivation and capacity to perform adequately. They are also seen as closed to new ideas, rigid, and dog-

---

[4]W. Lippman, *Public Opinion* (New York: Harcourt Brace Jovanovich, 1922), p. 81.

matic. Positive job-related age stereotypes depict older workers as honest, stable, and trustworthy.

Research evidence comparing the actual performance of younger and older workers shows quite consistently that job-related stereotypes are not valid. Individual differences within each age category overshadow performance differences attributable to age. Although the incidence of health problems does increase with age, in many instances there is no significant impairment of the ability of older workers to function in a variety of positions across the occupational spectrum. Contrary to age stereotypes, older workers often have much better attendance and accident records than do their younger counterparts.

Depictions of the elderly as impoverished, uninvolved, inactive, and out of touch are erroneous. A large percentage of older people desire employment or opportunities to participate in government, religious, political, or voluntary organizations.

Age stereotypes serve a number of psychological functions and are therefore quite resistant to change. Yet the retention of inaccurate age stereotypes will lead to a wasteful underutilization of valued resources. Public policymakers and corporate human resource planners face the challenge of creating new societal and organizational roles that capture the energy, experience, and wisdom of our nation's senior citizens. The challenge was most eloquently stated by Representative Claude Pepper, on his 81st birthday, when he opened the meeting of the U.S. House of Representatives Select Committee on Aging:

> Competence, not age, should determine whether a person may keep a job. To do otherwise is to squander one of our nation's most precious resources and to hasten the day of the end of those who are denied the experience that would keep them vitally and for a long time alive.

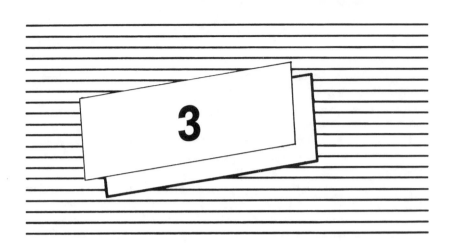

How Age
Stereotypes Influence
Managerial Decisions[1]

Main Issues

- Research evidence shows that managers must guard against stereotyped treatment of older employees in training and development, job assignment, and promotion.

- Research evidence also shows that the vast majority of managers are aware of the need for enlightened policies on older employees.

- Stereotypes and their effects are not easily overcome. Special efforts are required.

[1]This chapter is based on Benson Rosen and Thomas H. Jerdee, "Too Old or Not Too Old," *Harvard Business Review* 55, no. 6 (November–December 1977), pp. 97–106. Copyright © 1977 by the President and Fellows of Harvard College. All rights reserved.

Managers need to have some standards, yardsticks, or criteria for judging employees when making personnel decisions. There are many widely accepted judgmental criteria, such as technical competence, skills, experience, and past performance. Sometimes, however, managers may base their judgments on a different, unconscious standard. This standard is employee age, and it creeps into judgments because of assumptions about the inability of older employees to perform as well as younger employees in many jobs. In this chapter, we describe findings from our research, conducted with the cooperation of the *Harvard Business Review*, that clearly show how unconscious age stereotypes influence day-to-day managerial decisions. We conclude that a significant underutilization of human resources results when older workers are treated in terms of negative age stereotypes. In later chapters, we suggest how managers can enhance and extend the productive contributions of older employees.

A Research Strategy

In the preceding chapter, we examined the nature of job-related age stereotypes—that is, widely held beliefs about the capacities and limitations of people in various age categories. Stereotypical views depict older workers as potentially less employable than younger persons, particularly for managerial positions. Research findings suggest that older persons are seen as less capable of responding creatively, enthusiastically, or efficiently to job demands. Moreover, age stereotypes depict older employees as less interested in change and less capable of coping with future challenges. To the extent that these stereotypes influence managerial decisions, there are potentially serious consequences for older employees, including lowered motivation, career stagnation, and eventual career obsolescence. To determine the extent to which age stereotypes creep into administrative decisions, we conducted a questionnaire survey of *Harvard Business Review* readers.

The survey questions were embedded in a decision-making exercise. We asked the participants to assume an administrative role in a fictitious organization and to make decisions about a series of problem incidents that were presented in letter or memo form. There were two versions of each incident, one featuring an older person and the other a younger one. Each participant received only one version of each incident and was not aware that many others were reading the same incident with a different-aged person. The participants indicated how they would handle each incident by evaluating several approaches for resolving the managerial problem.

The incidents were comparable to many one-of-a-kind problems that practicing managers encounter where no clear-cut organizational rules or precedents exist to guide managerial actions, such as how to deal with an errant worker or correct a compensation inequity. We hypothesized that in such instances managers were particularly susceptible to the influence of age stereotypes. Each incident required the reader to take decisive managerial action on the basis of only limited information, and for only one employee, thus involving no direct comparison between younger and older employees.

In these situations, where direct comparison was not possible, we expected that managers would not be sensitized to the possibilities of age discrimination. On the other hand, had we depicted situations where direct age comparisons were involved, we would have expected managers to be sensitized to the dangers of age discrimination, in which case they would have been less likely to let age influence their decisions.

The use of two forms of the survey questionnaire permitted us to examine the impact of age stereotypes on managerial decisions without directly calling attention to the age factor. Details of the research approach are summarized in the following section.

The Survey Approach

The survey questionnaire was presented to *Harvard Business Review* subscribers, who were asked to assume the role of a "troubleshooter" charged with the responsibility of making decisions and resolving problems related to a recent organizational expansion. In the troubleshooter role, the participants responded to eight memos or letters depicting a variety of organizational problems, recommending appropriate action for each incident.

The specific contents of the exercise were as follows:

1. A hypothetical organization, FEDCO, was described, and the survey participants were instructed to assume the role of a manager in a newly created division.

2. Incidents depicting various personnel problems associated with staffing and managing the new division were presented.

3. There was a younger person version and an older person version for seven of the incidents. For example, some participants evaluated the qualifications of a 32-year-old applicant for a marketing position, while others evaluated an identically qualified 61-year-old applicant for the same position.

    The incidents featured average or marginal employees rather than extremely well qualified or unqualified employees. (Previous research had shown that managers were more likely to be influenced by stereotypes when dealing with average employees.)

    To enhance the realism of the decision exercise and to increase the salience of the employee's age, we included personnel forms with pictures of the key employees in five of the memos. The pictures were of uniformly attractive younger or older men and women dressed in business attire.

4. The final item in the exercise was a "mini" opinion survey designed to assess the participants' attitudes toward various policy issues, including policies regarding the employment of older employees.

5. Two complete questionnaires were assembled. Form 1 featured a younger employee in the first incident, an older employee in the second incident, and so forth. Form 2 depicted an older employee in the first incident, a younger employee in the second incident, and so forth. Since each participant in the survey received only one form of the questionnaire and was unaware of the existence of an alternative form, the manipulation of employees' ages was not obvious.

6. For each item, the participants indicated on scales the extent to which they would find certain administrative actions appropriate for dealing with the managerial problems. Many of these were six-point scales ranging from strongly unfavorable to strongly favorable. (The percentages reported are summed over the three favorable categories.)

7. Analysis of the influence of age stereotypes on managerial decisions was made by comparing the responses for the younger person and older person versions of each incident.

TABLE 3-1

Profile of *Harvard Business Review* Survey Participants

Age				
Under 30	11.7%	Banking, investment, insurance	11.2
30–34	18.8	Construction, mining, oil	4.0
35–39	19.2	Defense or space industry	3.5
40–44	15.0	Education, social services	6.1
45–49	15.2	Government	5.4
50–54	9.7	Management consulting	4.2
55–59	6.7	Retail or wholesale trade	7.7
60–64	2.9	Personal consumer service	1.0
65 and over	0.7	Transportation, public utility	4.3
Geographic area		Other	13.4
Northeast	11.2%		
Middle Atlantic	20.0	**Functional area**	
Middle West	26.2	Accounting	5.5%
Southeast	13.3	Engineering	7.0
South Central	10.0	Finance	8.6
Mountain	4.0	General management	42.6
Far West	14.9	Marketing	14.8
		Personnel	7.1
Kind of organization		Production	4.0
Manufacturing, consumer goods	12.0%	Public relations	1.0
		Other	9.3
Manufacturing, industrial goods	24.6	**Sex**	
Advertising, media, publishing	2.6	Male	93.0%
		Female	7.0

8.   Either Form 1 or Form 2 of the survey was sent to a national sample of 6,000 *Harvard Business Review* readers. Approximately 26 percent (1,570) returned the survey forms, with almost equal numbers returning each form.

Table 3–1 gives a profile of the respondents. The participants included a cross section of managers from a variety of industries and job functions.

Survey Findings: Influence of Age Stereotypes on Disciplinary Actions, Career Development, and Promotion Decisions

The responses to the survey suggested that, because of managerial actions based on age stereotypes, older employees are potential victims of unjust treatment. Specifically:

Managers perceive older employees to be relatively inflexible and resistant to change. Accordingly, managers make much less effort to give older persons feedback about needed changes in performance.

Managers provide very limited organizational support for the career development and retraining of older employees.

The promotion opportunities for older people are somewhat restricted, particularly when the new positions demand creativity, mental alertness, or the capacity to deal with crisis situations.

When asked directly for their opinions in regard to management policies for older employees, the participants favored greater affirmative action efforts, including the elimination of mandatory retirement policies and the complete vesting of pensions. This suggests that the differential treatment of older and younger employees in the in-basket decisions was the result of the respondents' unconscious age stereotypes rather than conscious discrimination.

Management Responses to Specific Incidents

Although the questionnaire offered seven incidents (of which there were two versions), we will discuss only three of them in detail, as the other four touched on aspects of the same issues.

The Tedious Old Fool.   One incident examined the stereotype that older people are rigid in their work attitudes as well as resistant to change. The incident depicted an older shipping department employee who was unresponsive to customer calls for service. The problem employee was described in the accompanying memorandum.

(In the other version, the employee was depicted as younger, but his experience was described in identical terms.)

Memorandum

To: Director, METRO Division
From: Sales Manager
Subject: Customer Complaints

I am sure you will recall that, when you appointed me as sales manager, you also emphasized that this was a sales-oriented, customer-oriented business, and you advised me to come straight to you whenever I felt that other departments were not giving sufficient support to our sales staff. We have now encountered such a situation, and it seems to be centered on one individual, Alan Garfield, supervisor of our shipping department.

Basically, what it amounts to is that our customers cannot get their inquiries about shipments answered satisfactorily. We have followed the practice of establishing a direct link between customers and the shipping department, so that customers can get the fastest and most accurate information possible on the status of their shipments. This always worked well, until Garfield took over the department. Now, when anybody calls in with a question or complaint about a shipment, the people on Garfield's staff always switch the call to him, after which there is an annoyingly long wait. Then Garfield finally gets on the line and gives a complex, detailed explanation of shipping department problems, ending with a lecture on customer patience.

As you know, Garfield is an older employee, with many years of service in this company but only three months' experience in the shipping department job. His previous experience was in the credit department, purchasing department, and mail room.

When we promoted him to the job last fall, I attempted to impress on him the importance of being tactful with complaining customers, but it doesn't seem to have done any good. I would appreciate it if you would get this situation remedied as soon as possible, in order to ensure that our customers obtain satisfactory services from the shipping department.

The respondents were asked how difficult it would be to correct the ineffective behavior and what approach they would take in dealing with the problem. Their reactions to the problem are shown in Figure 3–1.

The managers who responded to the younger employee version of this problem saw much less difficulty in changing the employee. Furthermore, the respondents took very different administrative approaches to this problem, depending on the age of the problem employee. A positive corrective strategy, "a talk in which you encourage Garfield to change," was selected by a majority of the managers who read the younger version, but a much smaller proportion of the participants who received the older version recommended this approach. On the other hand, a majority of the managers who read the older version endorsed the strategy "suggest that he have someone else handle the calls."

Clearly, the respondents saw the older employee as more resistant to managerial influences, even though there was no evidence in the memorandum to support such a perception. Thus, rather than encourage an older person to improve his performance, a majority of the participants recommended avoiding a confrontation and instead reassigning the older employee.

What many managers may fail to realize, however, is that the decision to reassign the older employee, based on the assumption that he is inflexible, deprives the employee of an opportunity to improve his performance. In cases such as this, the effects of age stereotypes are difficult to overcome. By transferring the older employee, the manager avoids a direct test of his own assumptions about the person's rigidity and resistance to change and, in so doing, precludes the possibility of learning that the age stereotype is not valid.

FIGURE 3-1

Customer Complaints

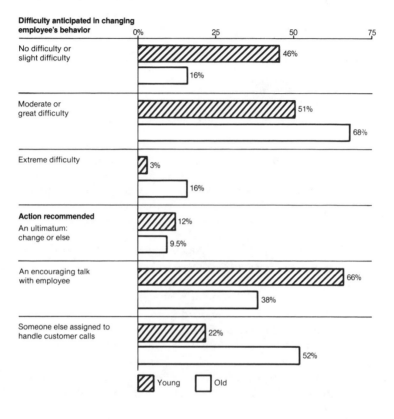

An Old Man Is Twice a Child.   Older employees, particularly those in technical positions, are vulnerable to problems of career obsolescence. In order to keep older employees' knowledge and skills up to date, they and management both need to have a commitment to continuous career development.

The next incident examined managerial assumptions about the decline in older employees' interest, motivation, and ability to improve their job-related skills.

The problem was described as follows: Ralph Adams, 63, has a two-year certificate in industrial technology. He has been a member of the production staff for 10 years. With the company's recent expansion, he was assigned from FEDCO's main offices to the new METRO Division. He has worked on routine assignments in time study and production scheduling. His performance evaluations have been "satisfactory."

(In the other version, the background information depicted a 34-year-old member of the production staff and was accompanied by a photograph of a younger man.)

Memorandum

To: Director, METRO Division
From: Ralph Adams
Subject: Production Seminar in Atlanta

I would like to attend the production seminar later this month in Atlanta. Several other members of the production staff, including one new employee, have attended similar seminars during the last few years. I feel that participants can learn about new theories and research relevant to production systems at these conferences. The conference is scheduled for two weeks, October 6–17. Please let me know as soon as possible.

(Note: The company policy has been to pay full salary and all expenses for employees who are selected to attend conferences. Since the budget for such activities is limited and many requests come in each year, division directors must be very careful whom they select.)

The participants evaluated the production employee's motivation for requesting training funds as well as the desirability of sending the employee to the training seminar. The responses to this case are shown in Figure 3–2.

A considerably larger proportion of the respondents perceived the younger employee to be concerned with keeping up with the latest production technology. A somewhat larger proportion of the respondents saw the older employee as concerned with securing a fair share of the training budget.

Managerial actions clearly favored the career development of the younger employee. About three fourths of the respondents who read the younger version of this case recommended that funds be allocated so that the employee could attend the training seminar, but only about half of the respondents who read the older version favored company support for training. Moreover, the participants recommended a decision to deny the request significantly more often for the older employee.

This case illustrates how managers' assumptions about the motivation of older workers to improve their job-related skills are reflected in their decisions to avoid investments in the continued development of older employees. Assumptions about retirement practices might also have influenced the responses. Administrators may view investments in the development of older persons as yielding fewer organizational benefits, compared with similar expenditures for the promotion and development

FIGURE 3–2

Production Seminar

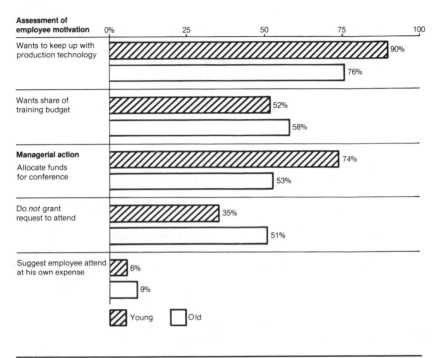

Assessment of employee motivation

| | 0% | 25 | 50 | 75 | 100 |

Wants to keep up with production technology — 90% (Young), 76% (Old)

Wants share of training budget — 52% (Young), 58% (Old)

Managerial action
Allocate funds for conference — 74% (Young), 53% (Old)

Do *not* grant request to attend — 35% (Young), 51% (Old)

Suggest employee attend at his own expense — 6% (Young), 9% (Old)

Young / Old

of younger employees. The validity of these assumptions depends on actual turnover rates among younger and older employees.

In a similar incident, which examined managerial reactions to an employee whose skills had become outdated, the participants were asked to evaluate strategies for handling the case. A higher percentage of the respondents were prepared to retrain the younger employee at the company's expense. The pattern of responses suggests that managers are somewhat reluctant to invest in the retraining of older persons, yet feel an obligation not to terminate their employment.

When considered together, the findings from these incidents suggest that managers are less likely to see older employees as motivated to keep up with the latest technology, and thus are less enthusiastic about providing retraining opportunities for older employees whose job knowledge has become obsolete. This puts older employees in a "Catch-22" predicament, trapped as double victims of age stereotypes. This predicament was manifested in a recent court case involving age discrimination in a supervisory training program. A manager for the company was on record as saying flatly, "You can't teach an old dog new tricks." Needless to say, the company lost the case.

They Have a Plentiful Lack of Wit.   The next incident tested the hypothesis that older employees are seen as less promotable to a position requiring creative and innovative thinking.

In the alternative forms of this case, the participants evaluated either a 61-year-old man or an identically qualified 32-year-old man for a marketing position.

Memorandum

To: Director, METRO Division
From: Assistant Director of Marketing, HQ
Subject: Marketing Director for METRO

I have followed up on your suggestion that we see if any of our marketing representatives are qualified for promotion to the Marketing Director's job at METRO. There is one candidate, Lawrence Evans, who might be suitable for this position. He has been with FEDCO for about six years, and during that time he has done a good job on somewhat routine assignments.

Would you please review this information and give us a verdict as soon as possible? If we have to go outside to fill this position, it might take us quite a while to find suitable recruits.

Please bear in mind that this is a responsible position that calls for a high degree of creativity and innovative thinking. We need a person who can develop fresh solutions to challenging problems involving buyers, designers, and our own marketing staff. Moreover, we need a farsighted person who can predict consumer tastes.

Evans has been a member of our Central Division staff for about six years, and his performance during that time has been favorable. His supervisor reports that he is a competent, methodical person. Before joining our company, Evans' experience was in retail sales, preceded by a civilian job on a Navy base. He is 61 years old, married, and has a son and a daughter.

The responses to this incident are shown in Figure 3–3. The participants rated the outlook for successful performance in the marketing position as much less favorable for the older candidate and indicated very little support for promoting him. Perhaps job demands requiring "fresh solutions to challenging problems" were incongruent with the participants' stereotypical views about the creative abilities of an older person.

A second case in which an employee was presented for promotion examined the stereotype that connects age with nervousness and declining mental alertness. The participants were asked to judge, first, whether a new supervisory position ought to be created and, second, whether a can-

FIGURE 3-3

Promotion to Marketing Director

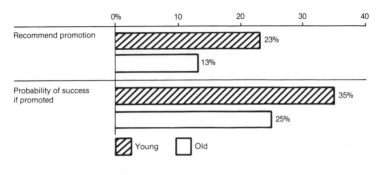

didate was suitable for the challenging new position. The majority favored the creation of a new supervisory position for the employee. However, the participants viewed the younger employee as more suitable for the new role and more likely to be recommended for promotion.

When we consider these two promotion cases together, we see a consistent pattern emerging. Older employees are seen as less able to cope with higher-level supervisory and managerial positions when role requirements conflict with age stereotypes. Therefore, the probability of a promotion is somewhat lower for an older employee than for an identically qualified younger person.

Clearly, an older employee has fewer career options than his or her younger counterpart. However, systematic exclusion of older employees from promotion opportunities can create problems of career stagnation. Since the older employee's mobility outside the organization is already restricted because of age, blocking opportunities for career advancement within the organization can lead the older person to conclude that satisfactory performance is no longer sufficient for or instrumental to career advancement. After being passed over, he or she may tend to behave so as to confirm managerial judgments of unpromotability, thus further strengthening the stereotypes.

An incident involving a branch manager who protested inequitable compensation further illustrates the limited mobility of older employees. When asked to estimate the absolute minimum salary increase that would be required to retain the branch manager, the participants recommended an average monthly increase of $100 for the younger manager, compared with an average monthly increase of only $85 for the older manager. Since managers perceive that an older employee will settle for less than a younger one, a vigorous demand from an older employee might result in the manager giving him a low adjustment on a take-it-or-leave-it basis.

When asked for their actual salary recommendations, however, the participants suggested slightly over $100 for both the younger employee and the older employee. Even though the survey respondents recognized the older employee's vulnerability, they were willing to rectify the salary inequity regardless of the employee's age. Apparently, advanced age was not seen as justification for compensation inequity in the context of this situation.

Mini Opinion Survey

The final in-basket item was a "mini" opinion survey. This item provided a means to assess directly managerial attitudes toward policies and practices affecting older employees.

The participants indicated their opinions in response to the accompanying letter, which was completely identical in all questionnaires.

Director, METRO Division
FEDCO Corporate Headquarters
Metropolis, USA

Dear Director:

I am writing you on behalf of the 1976 Panel of Advisers of the National Directors' Conference Board. As you know, each of us on the Panel has agreed to contribute his views on a number of policy issues during the current year. Our research subcommittee has approved the attached questionnaire as an efficient means of gathering your views. Your response will be appreciated.

Sincerely,

Robert Hudson
Chairman

The opinion survey data are summarized in Table 3–2. The responses reflect the participants' concern with the plight of the older employee as well as their support for implementing new policies designed to encourage expanded career opportunities for the elderly. For example, 31 percent of the participants felt that current business practices with respect to the treatment of older employees were inadequate, and 77 percent favored greater emphasis on affirmative action programs for older people. These

TABLE 3-2

National Directors' Opinion Survey Findings

1. Which of the following current business practices do you find inadequate?

Treatment of older employees	31%
Treatment of female employees	33
Health and safety of employees	12

2. Should there be greater emphasis on affirmative action for the following?

Older workers	77%
Females	72
Blacks	63

3. Which organizational policies do you agree with?

Complete vesting of pension plans	80%
Elimination of mandatory retirement ages (at 65 or earlier)	60
Flexible work schedules for hourly employees	61
Profit sharing for all employees	81
Company-provided day care	40

findings reflect managerial sensitivity to the status of the older employee compared with that of other groups.

A great majority of the survey participants indicated that they favored reforms in policies governing the employment of older employees. Thus 80 percent of the participants supported a policy of complete vesting of pension plans, a reform that would do much to increase the career options of older employees. Moreover, 60 percent favored elimination of mandatory retirement at age 65. Organizational criteria for the retention of all employees could then be made on the basis of individual differences in performance, health, and motivation rather than on the basis of an arbitrarily set chronological age limit.

Responses of Older Participants

In further analyses of the survey sample according to the respondents' age, the reactions of 302 respondents in the age 50 and over group are of particular interest. In general, the responses of this group of participants seem to reflect greater concern for problems of career obsolescence and stagnation. For example, respondents in the over-50 age category were more likely to recommend financial support to enable an older employee to attend a technical seminar. In the incident involving a computer programmer whose skills had become outdated, 85 percent of the older respondents, compared with 73 percent of the younger respondents, recommended that the company sponsor retraining for a 60-year-old programmer.

In promotion decisions, the older respondents were much less likely to be influenced by the candidate's age. These respondents were equally likely to promote both the younger and the older man for a marketing position, and they favored the creation of a new supervisory position for both a younger and an older woman. Similarly, the older respondents were equally pessimistic about changing the behavior of both a younger and an older shipping department employee.

The pattern of responses to the remaining in-basket incidents and to the opinion questionnaire was identical for respondents in all age categories.

In summary, for an older employee, the best prospects for fair and perhaps favored treatment appear to be in working for an older boss.

Prospects for Change

Age stereotypes clearly influenced managerial decisions in many of the experimental in-basket incidents. In one incident, the respondents viewed an older worker as more rigid and resistant to change, and they were therefore more inclined to transfer him rather than to help him overcome a problem. Similarly, the respondents would retain but not retrain an older employee whose skills had become obsolete. There was also a tendency to withhold promotions from older workers where identically qualified younger workers would be granted promotions.

For some incidents, however, there was no evidence of age stereotyping in the responses. The participants showed no age stereotyping in redressing a compensation inequity. Nor was there any evidence to suggest that the respondents would pressure older employees to resign or accept early retirement. However, when managers retain older employees but deny them opportunities for development and promotion, they relegate them to a position of "marking time" until retirement.

The commonly accepted belief that older employees reach a point in their careers when motivation declines significantly and they merely "go through the motions" until retirement is perhaps due in part to organizationally created self-fulfilling prophecies. Managers who expect a decline in motivation among older workers might make age-based managerial decisions that in fact lead to decreased motivation for these employees. To the extent that an older employee perceives that his efforts are no longer linked to organizational advancement, his motivation may gradually decline.

Limited opportunities for development and lack of feedback about performance may further reduce the older employee's motivation. Thus it is likely that lowered motivation may result, not from aging itself, but from managerial expectations and treatment of older employees.

There was an intriguing discrepancy between the participants' expressed attitudes of concern for older workers on the opinion survey questions and their decisions in response to the in-basket items. Some of the respondents may have believed that less favorable treatment of an older worker was justified by the circumstances in some of the in-basket incidents. For example, some respondents may have assumed a shorter work-life expectancy for people close to retirement age, which would imply a shorter payback period for an investment in training.

While this may seem to be a reasonable assumption, it poses problems for older employees, especially in times of rapid change, when continuing development of skills is particularly important to performance. Thus management is challenged to reconcile its concerns for fair treatment of older workers with the undeniably short work-life expectancies of these employees. In considering this problem, managers might also bear in mind the problem of turnover among younger employees.

Another interpretation of the discrepancy between attitudes and decisions is that the participants, although favoring policy changes to broaden career options for older employees, were unknowingly influenced by their own unconscious age stereotypes in responding to the in-basket incidents. If this interpretation is correct, policy changes to eliminate discrimination against older employees represent only a first step. Additional efforts will be required to help managers identify age stereotypes and eliminate their effects on everyday decisions, which ought to be made on the basis of individual qualifications and should not be influenced by employee membership in a particular age category.

These efforts must deal not only with the stereotypes themselves but also with a number of other items that tend to support and perpetuate the stereotypes. The other items include the following:

1. *Pension constraints.* Under current pension formulas, retirement benefits may become increasingly expensive when high-salaried employees are retained beyond mandatory retirement. The same may become true of medical benefit costs, under a current government proposal to remove employed older persons from medicare.

2. *Pressures to promote women and minority employees.* In order to create openings at higher levels, organizations may choose to avail themselves of early and mandatory retirement policies. University administrators have been especially prone to this viewpoint.

3. *Self-interest.* Many managers may see it as in their own self-interest to make more room at the top by sticking to inflexible retirement policies.

4. *Evaluation avoidance.* Having to evaluate the fitness of others for continued employment, or having to undergo such evaluation oneself, is uncomfortable.
5. *Weak enforcement of age discrimination legislation.* The enforcement mechanisms necessary to protect the rights of older employees have only recently been set into motion and have not yet been perfected.
6. *Lack of organized representation.* Some older employees do not have a powerful advocacy organization. Victims of arbitrary forced retirement policies often have to fend for themselves against their employers, a situation in which many older employees perceive themselves as helpless.

The economic realities of an aging work force make policy changes inevitable. Faced with a shrinking ratio of working to retired persons, our society will soon be forced to consider alternatives to mandatory retirement, including more emphasis on part-time work and flexible working hours and on gradual or phased retirement for older people. We address each of these changes in human resource policies in the following chapters. The idea that careers should end at a fixed chronological age is long overdue for "retirement."

4

Age Discrimination Law

Main Issues

- The Age Discrimination in Employment Amendments of 1978 (ADEA) prohibit discrimination on the basis of age in employment practices, for persons between the ages of 40 and 70.

- Litigation under ADEA is increasing.

- The most frequent issue under ADEA is discriminatory termination.

- The penalties and legal costs for violations can be severe.

- Lack of intent to discriminate is not an adequate defense.

- The best defense is a systematic program of human resource management, including career planning for all ages, careful performance assessment, good feedback and counseling, and flexible retirement provisions.

- Complete abolition of mandatory retirement seems imminent but is unlikely to cause major disruptions.

What are the legal issues surrounding the employment of older workers? Can a company fire an employee over age 40 without fear of a lawsuit? What changes can be expected in legislation regulating mandatory retirement, pension contributions, and medical benefits for older workers?

In this chapter, we take a careful look at the legal issues related to the employment of older workers. Case examples illustrate recent interpretations of the 1967 Age Discrimination in Employment Act and the 1978 amendments extending mandatory retirement to age 70. We conclude with a glimpse at proposed legislation calling for the complete abolition of mandatory retirement.

Background on ADEA

In the mid-1960s, President Lyndon Johnson expressed concern about the increasing numbers of older workers who were not yet ready for retirement but were unable to find jobs. In a special message to Congress proposing programs for older workers, President Johnson noted that "hundreds of thousands not yet old, not yet voluntarily retired find themselves jobless because of arbitrary age discrimination." He argued that "in addition to the shameful waste of human resources, the older worker problem costs the country millions of dollars in unemployment insurance and welfare payments." According to Johnson, a federal policy designed to help workers over age 40 was clearly needed.

1967 ADEA

In order to ensure equal employment opportunities for older workers, President Johnson signed into law the Age Discrimination in Employment Act (ADEA) on December 15, 1967. The thrust of the legislation was two-fold: (1) protection of workers from age discrimination between the ages of 40 and 65 and (2) promotion of employment opportunities for older workers capable of meeting job requirements.

Amendments

The 1967 ADEA was amended in 1974 to include coverage of government employees at the local, state, and federal level. It was amended again in 1978 to advance coverage to age 70 and to abolish mandatory retirement altogether for federal employees.

Coverage

Recent Labor Department statistics estimate that about 28 million persons are protected by the ADEA umbrella. This amounts to 70 percent of Americans aged 40–79 in the civilian labor force.

As amended, the act regulates the employment practices of private and public employers, employment agencies, and labor organizations. Specifically falling under the act are:

Private employers of 20 or more persons.

Public employers at the federal, state, and local government level (except for certain elected officials and their appointees and advisers).

Labor organizations if they are engaged in an industry "affecting interstate commerce." Labor unions are included under the act if they (1) recruit and hire workers for employers or (2) have 25 or more members and (a) are certified as a bargaining agent under the Taft-Hartley Act or Railway Labor Act or (b) are otherwise recognized as bargaining agents by employers or (c) have some formal relationship with a covered union, such as a joint council membership with a covered union.

Employment agencies that regularly, with or without compensation, undertake to recruit, select, and refer employees for an employer.

Prohibitions

Specific prohibitions are spelled out in Section 4 of the act. It is a violation of the act for employers: (1) to fail or refuse to hire, to discharge, or in other ways to discriminate against any individual with respect to compensation, or other terms or conditions of employment, because of age; (2) to limit, segregate, or classify employees in a way that might deprive any individual of employment opportunities, or adversely affect his or her status as an employee, because of age; (3) to reduce the wage rate of any employee because of age.

Employment agency practices are also regulated by the act. It is against the law for employment agencies to fail or refuse to refer for employment or otherwise discriminate against any individual because of age or to classify or refer anyone for employment on the basis of age.

Labor organizations are prohibited from (1) discrimination because of age by excluding or expelling any individual from membership; by limiting, segregating, or classifying their members on the basis of age; or by other means; (2) failing or refusing to refer anyone for employment so as to deprive or limit employment opportunities or otherwise limit an individual's status because of age; and (3) causing or attempting to cause an employer to discriminate against any individual because of age.

Employers, employment agencies, and labor organizations are prohibited from harassing workers who in any way question the legality of current practices with respect to the act. Specifically, Section 4(d) of the act states that it is unlawful for an employer to discriminate against any of his employees or applicants for employment, for an employment agency to discriminate against any individual, or for a labor organization to discriminate against any member or applicant for membership because that individual has opposed any unlawful practice or has made a charge or assisted in an investigation, proceeding, or litigation under the act.

Advertisement for members, employees, or clients is regulated under Section 4(e) of the act. The use of printed or published notices or advertisements indicating any preference, limitation, specification, or discrimination based on age is prohibited.

Exceptions

Although the ADEA is very comprehensive, certain prohibitions against age discrimination do not apply. For example, an individual's age can be considered in employment decisions when the employer can show that age is a bona fide occupational qualification, reasonably necessary to the normal operations of a business. Note, however, that establishment of this exception is not easy. Organizational practices such as the setting of maximum age limits on hiring must be substantiated with proof that age requirements are essential for the protection of the public or on the basis of some other reasonable business necessity.

Differential treatment of employees based on reasonable factors other than age, such as physical fitness, is permitted. Nothing in the act precludes the discharge or discipline of an older worker for good cause. Careful documentation may be critical if an age discrimination suit is filed, as discussed later in this chapter.

Enforcement

When the ADEA was originally enacted, the secretary of labor was charged with enforcement responsibility. Now the responsibility for enforcement falls under the jurisdiction of the Equal Employment Opportunity Commission (EEOC).

Litigation Procedures

Complaints of alleged age discrimination are first filed with the EEOC. Representatives of the EEOC notify the prospective defendants of the charges and attempt through informal methods of conciliation or persuasion to effect voluntary compliance with the act. The conciliation process is designed to speed up the resolution of complaints, a critical consideration for out-of-work employees.

In cases where conciliation fails, the EEOC or any individual may initiate a lawsuit. The 1978 amendments authorize the option of a jury trial in cases where the alleged discrimination involves potential monetary liabilities such as back pay.

The burden of proof in an age discrimination suit initially falls on the alleged victim. He or she must establish a prima facie case by showing membership in the protected group (age 40–69) and by documenting that he or she was denied an employment opportunity that was later granted to an equally qualified or less qualified younger person.

The defendant, an employer or a prospective employer, then has the opportunity to answer the charges of age discrimination. In many instances, employers attempt to justify their personnel actions on the basis of one of the ADEA exception clauses, such as business necessity. For example, an employer might defend a personnel decision on the ground that the older employee could not meet performance standards or that the older employee's declining functional abilities represented a potential threat to the public safety.

Once an initial defense has been offered by the defendant, the burden of proof again shifts to the alleged victim. The plaintiff must convince a jury that the most reasonable inference to be drawn from the circumstances and from the evidence presented is that age discrimination has occurred.

Penalties

Judgments sustaining age discrimination charges can prove very costly, often requiring compensation, back pay, and reinstatement. Under the ADEA, an individual may sue for payment plus attorneys' fees and court costs. Where willful violations have been proven, an additional amount owed may be claimed as liquidated damages.

Past court decisions help define what can be recovered for violations. A number of federal district courts have ruled in favor of awarding compensatory damages for pain and suffering. For example, in 1977 the National Cash Register Company was ordered to pay $15,000 to two discharged employees as compensation for the embarrassment and the disruption of their lives that resulted from their discharge.

In enforcement actions, the courts are authorized to grant any relief appropriate to carry out the act's purposes, including judgments compelling employment, reinstatement, or promotion. The case of *Rodriguez* v. *Taylor* represents an interesting example of court action to grant relief. In this case, the court awarded back pay to an "unqualified" job applicant. The back pay award was made to compensate the job applicant for uncertainty experienced during a period of time when he had been prevented from taking a civil service examination because he was over age 40.

Increased Litigation

Litigation brought under ADEA has increased significantly since it was first enacted. Back in 1967, age discrimination was pretty much a nonissue; in that year, the Department of Labor filed only one age bias case. By 1974, 3,040 age discrimination complaints had been filed, and more than 180 court cases were in the works. In 1981, the EEOC received 9,479 age discrimination complaints. Most experts agree that with an aging work force further increases in the number of age bias suits are quite likely.

If size of financial settlement is an indicator of the impact of ADEA suits, employers are forewarned not to take lightly legislation protecting the rights of older workers. Through 1972, the largest age discrimination settlement involved Pan American Airways, which was ordered to pay $250,000 to 29 former employees. In 1974, the Labor Department reached a $2 million settlement with Standard Oil of California. In 1982 and 1983, Consolidated Edison Company of New York settled an age discrimination case by agreeing to pay former employees $3.7 million in back wages and extra pension benefits, Liggett & Myers Tobacco Company agreed to pay $7 million in back wages and lost benefits to 107 employees as a result of an age discrimination suit, and United Air Lines was ordered to pay 114 pilots and engineers $18 million in an age discrimination suit.

In one of the largest suits to date, a former General Motors executive with 23 years of experience is seeking $69 million in damages, claiming that he was fired because of his age. According to GM, the executive was replaced as a result of a major reorganization aimed at revamping the marketing effort.

In a recent government survey, 8 out of 10 employers predicted a significant increase in the number of age discrimination lawsuits in the near future. Legal experts agree that the trend toward increasing age discrimination litigation will continue. They also expect such litigation to be directed in particular against companies experiencing fierce competition. In these companies, long-term survival depends on clearing out unproductive employees. When workers feel that terminations on this ground are unjust, litigation results. In fact, the greatest number of age discrimination charges have come from terminated men in the 50–59 age category. A majority of these men held managerial or supervisory positions. While charges of age discrimination have been widespread in all industries, they have been particularly frequent in the manufacturing, service, and wholesale-retail industries.

According to an attorney who has handled 300 age discrimination cases, corporations underestimate the degree to which they can get hurt in age discrimination litigation. Another attorney specializing in bias suits noted, "One aim of the big back pay awards is to make employers think twice before firing older workers."

While the costs to business of age discrimination lawsuits have been great, the costs of age discrimination to society have been even greater. Labor economists estimate that nearly 2 million person-years of productive time are lost each year because of unemployment among older workers. And the unemployment insurance benefits paid to older workers exceed $2.2 billion annually.

Given the increasing frequency of age discrimination litigation, the growing magnitude of the financial settlements in such litigation, and the staggering social costs of age discrimination, it seems imperative that managers have a clear understanding of the regulations governing the employment of older workers.

Types of Age Discrimination Charges

Age discrimination can take many forms. Computerized record keeping by the Equal Employment Opportunity Commission permits tabulation

TABLE 4-1

Type of Charge Filed with the EEOC in 1981

Type of Charge	Percent
Termination	49
Hiring	12
Terms and conditions	8
Wages and benefits	7
Promotion	5
Demotion	4
Training	1
All other	14

Source: Adapted from Claude Pepper, *Age Discrimination in Employment: A Growing Problem in America*, Select Committee on Aging, February 22, 1982 (Washington D.C.: U.S. Government Printing Office).

of age discrimination suits by the nature of the charge. Table 4–1 shows a complete breakdown of the complaints filed in 1981. Forced termination was the most frequent complaint.

What Constitutes Age Discrimination?

While the Age Discrimination in Employment Act appears clear and straightforward, in practice age discrimination may be difficult to identify and hard to prove. Consider the following cases:

A 60-year-old secretary with 30 years of experience cannot find employment. Is it because her secretarial skills have become rusty, or is it because of her age?

A research and development firm replaces a senior scientist with one fresh out of school. Has the scientist been replaced because of his research incompetence or because a recent college graduate is less expensive than a senior scientist?

A 58-year-old product manager for a major bread manufacturer is passed over for promotion in favor of a younger, less experienced colleague. Is the promotion lost because of age discrimination or because the manager's marketing ideas have gone stale?

Case Examples

Complex legislation regulating employment practices often requires interpretation by the courts. Since 1967, a body of case law in the area of age discrimination has emerged. In order to help managers become familiar with the interpretation and application of the ADEA, we present and discuss a series of hypothetical examples illustrating various features of the act. The examples are hypothetical, but they are based on actual court cases, so our discussion is indicative of past case outcomes.

Recruitment

Newspaper want ads that blatantly discriminate against older applicants are gradually disappearing. It wasn't very long ago, however, that the "Help Wanted" section of most newspapers contained such discriminatory wording as "student age 18–21," "salesman under 30," and "waitress 21–25." Equally discriminatory are advertisements that do not specify age per se but use such phrases as "junior secretary," "college student," "young woman," "boy," or "recent high school graduate." Advertisments that suggest preferences, qualifiers, or limitations based on age are almost always illegal.

Back in 1973, the Department of Labor surveyed newspaper help wanted advertisments and found 1,836 want ads placed by employers, employment agencies, and unions that violated the age discrimination law. An estimated 15,000 workers were likely victims of these illegal recruiting practices.

Often organizational recruiting practices can be the source of a more subtle type of age discrimination. Consider the following incident.

Case 1:   College Graduates

INSKO, a multinational corporation with offices in 11 countries, has a long-standing policy of recruiting college graduates for its future executive training program. An INSKO personnel officer typically visits the campuses of the top 20 business schools in the country. On the basis of recruiting interviews, about 25 college seniors are offered entry-level positions with INSKO. Upon joining INSKO after graduation, the new recruits are placed in a highly structured executive training program. The program consists of a series of job rotations, including foreign assignments and service on a junior board of directors in one of the major divisions. Successful graduates of the program frequently step up to middle-level management and administrative positions. The average age of program graduates is 27.

Discussion of Case 1

The INSKO recruitment and development policy appears to have great merit. Early identification of managerial talent coupled with intensive training and development experiences seems to be the formula for rapid progression in the organization. For all of its virtue, however, the INSKO personnel policy could be discriminatory.

At issue in this case is the access of older workers to entry-level positions and to the executive training program. Since age tends to be highly correlated with college graduation, the policy of recruiting future managers from the ranks of college seniors potentially discriminates against older employees with comparable credentials. INSKO would be particularly vulnerable to charges of age discrimination if admission to the executive training program were limited *exclusively* to recent college graduates. On the other hand, if employees of all ages who have demonstrated management potential are given consideration when it comes time to select executive trainees, then INSKO's recruitment and training policy is in compliance with the age discrimination act.

An ice cream company operating 380 restaurants in 11 states followed a recruitment policy similar to that depicted in Case 1. The Department of Labor charged that the company practice discriminated against older applicants for its management training program and required that the company establish an affirmative action policy for hiring older workers and pay $40,000 in lost wages to previously rejected job applicants. The outcome of this case suggests that strict enforcement of the ADEA may lead to questions regarding organizational hiring and promotion practices where management trainees are recruited exclusively from college graduating classes.

Selection

Age bias can also creep into personnel decisions involving the selection of new employees. Personnel officers who reject applicants over an arbitrarily determined age cutoff without consideration of their job qualifications are guilty of age discrimination. Professional employment agencies or executive search firms that fail to refer otherwise qualified candidates over age 40 are also in violation of the law. Similarly, union officials who pass over older members for job assignments are guilty of discrimination.

In some instances, organizational practices with respect to the recruitment and selection of new employees are influenced by other corporate policies, as depicted in the next case.

Case 2:   Youthful Image

Seans is a new restaurant franchise featuring a natural food menu. Extensive market research commissioned by the founders of Seans indicated that a potential market, untapped by the competition, was relatively young, dual-career families. Market research indicated that this group was willing to spend more for dinner than was usually required by hamburger and pizza chains. Accordingly, Seans targeted its advertising campaign to these young families.

The Seans image as conveyed by advertisements, restaurant decor, and even background music was tailored to appeal especially to a young and sophisticated market. The Seans personnel policies were designed to complement that image. Efforts were made to hire young, well-groomed men and women for hostess, cashier, and waitress positions.

Karen Hansen applied for a position as a hostess at a newly opened Seans. She had previous restaurant experience. The assistant personnel officer noted that she was pleasant and outgoing, two qualities required in Seans hostesses. Mrs. Hansen was rejected for the position, however. She was 49 years old. In the eyes of the personnel administrator, she just did not "fit" with the Seans image.

Discussion of Case 2

Was the personnel administrator's rejection of Karen Hansen a violation of the Age Discrimination in Employment Act? Clearly, the personnel administrator considered her age in this decision. The important issue here is whether age represents a bona fide occupational qualification for working as a hostess.

Age is a bona fide occupational qualification (bfoq) when it can be demonstrated that all or almost all individuals in a particular age category cannot meet the requirements for a specific job. In this instance, the Seans administrators would have to produce evidence that most or all applicants over a particular age (perhaps 40 in this example) were incapable of meeting the physical, mental, and interpersonal demands necessary to perform the job of hostess. Such proof seems extremely unlikely in this instance.

Organizational image or even customer preferences for attractive young hostesses would not be sufficient justification in most instances for rejecting an otherwise qualified 49-year-old job applicant. In an actual case involving a retail clothing store, the owners adopted a policy designed to appeal to a younger clientele. Six older sales employees who were discharged by the retailer successfully filed an age discrimination suit. The retailer was unable to defend the termination of the older workers on any rational business basis.[1]

For many years, the airlines considered only young, attractive, and single females for flight attendant positions. Some of the physical requirements for these positions could be justified in terms of easy movement through the narrow aisles of the aircraft. The age, sex, and marital status requirements, on the other hand, were primarily for show. Today flight attendants are a much more heterogeneous group. Since airline business is reaching record-high levels, it is clear that the previous age, sex, and marital status requirements were not crucial after all.

When is age a bona fide occupational qualification? The next case provides some insights.

Case 3:   Driver Safety

Transamerica Motors operates a bus system throughout the Southwest. Over the years, the company has compiled comprehensive statistics on driver safety. Analysis of the data indicated that drivers over age 45 had more accidents than younger drivers. Within the group of drivers over 45, however, a subgroup of drivers between ages 50 and 60 with 15 years of experience had the safest driving records in the company.

The vice president for personnel reasoned that it would be impossible for new drivers over age 35 to accumulate 15 years of experience before they reached what the company called the "high-risk age." He therefore felt that setting a maximum age of 35 as a criterion for selecting new drivers was justified.

A second consideration in setting maximum age limits for bus drivers was the seniority system for route assignments used by Transamerica. Drivers with seniority were given the option of selecting routes and schedules. Typically, senior drivers opted for less demanding routes, leaving the more rigorous and demanding routes to newly hired drivers. Extrapolating from the accident statistics, assignment of drivers over age 35 to the most difficult routes and schedules increased the risk of injury to Transamerica passengers.

The vice president for personnel consulted several medical authorities to determine whether accident proneness could be assessed in the context of a medical examination. They advised him that except in extreme cases it would be very difficult to predict physiological changes 5 or 10 years in the future. They noted that degenerative changes be-

---

[1]*Bishop v. Jelleff Associates* (DC D.C. 1974) 7EPD 9214.

gan at around age 35 and that some of these changes could gradually impair driving ability. They cautioned that changes in functional age were not perfectly correlated with changes in chronological age. In other words, some individuals would experience considerably slower reaction time at age 35 or 40, while others might experience little change in reaction time until a much older age.

After considering all of the evidence and medical advice, the vice president for personnel concluded that age was a bona fide occupational qualification for the selection of new bus drivers. The available statistical evidence indicated that all or almost all drivers over age 50 with less than 15 years of experience were more likely to be involved in an accident than were younger drivers. He therefore ordered the personnel department to select new drivers from the applicants who were under 35 years old.

Discussion of Case 3

Can an organization refuse to hire an applicant over 35 years old on the basis of statistical evidence about his predicted safety record? As we have pointed out, the burden of proof is on the employer to demonstrate that age is an occupational qualification necessary for normal operation of the enterprise.

In the Transamerica case, passenger safety would certainly be considered necessary for normal operations of the enterprise. Statistical evidence demonstrating the relationship of age to driver safety, coupled with the difficulty of diagnosing reduced driving capacity, would very likely be sufficient to support the claim that age is a bona fide occupational qualification in this instance.

Two actual cases, involving Greyhound Lines and Tamiami Trail Tours, tested the courts' interpretation of the Age Discrimination in Employment Act on the issue of age and passenger safety. In both cases, the U.S. court of appeals approved the use of age as a selection criterion for new drivers. In the *Tamiami* case, the court stated that age is a bona fide ocupational qualification necessary to satisfy the extraordinary burden placed on motor carriers for safety of their passengers and that chronological age is the best available tool for screening out bus driver applicants likely to be safety risks.[2]

Age is likely to be upheld as a bona fide occupational qualification in jobs with stringent physical demands. Accordingly, it is not uncommon to find age limits governing the selection and retirement of police officers, fire fighters, air traffic controllers, and persons in similar jobs where

---

[2]*Hodgson* v. *Tamiami Trail Tours, Inc.* (DC Fla. 1972) 4EPD 7795; aff'd (CA-5 1976) EPD 10, 916531 F.2d 224.

strenuous physical exertion or work under stressful conditions is required. The courts have been particularly willing to accept age criteria for positions where the public safety is involved.

It is dangerous, however, to make assumptions about physical incapacities associated with aging in the absence of statistical or medical data. A court of appeals ruled, for example, that age cannot be considered in determining the flight status of test pilots. In *Houghton v. McDonnell Douglas*, the court ruled that Houghton, a 52-year-old test pilot who had been transferred to a desk position, was the victim of arbitrary age discrimination.[3] Medical testimony and documentary evidence indicated age-related changes were much slower for test pilots than for the general population. In this instance, the appeals court acknowledged that "medical technology can predict a disabling physical condition in a test pilot with foolproof accuracy, and safety records of older professional pilots are better than those of younger ones due to their experience."

It appears that the decisions in the *Greyhound* and *McDonnell Douglas* cases are inconsistent. Differing conclusions in these two cases suggest that the interpretation of what constitutes a bfoq is not clear-cut. To a considerable extent, court decisions depend on the type and extent of objective evidence that can be presented in support of the employer's contention that a bfoq exists and justifies age discrimination.[4]

Retention

During business slowdowns or periods of economic recession, companies frequently face the necessity of making work force reductions. In many instances, decisions regarding which employees are to be retained are based on seniority. When retention policies are ambiguous and disproportionate numbers of older workers are laid off or terminated, a company may be suspected of possible age discrimination, as illustrated in the next case.

Case 4:   Hard Times Hit Harlow

Harlow Industries develops high-technology electronic components under contracts with the Air Force and NASA. Harlow's work force consists predominantly of scientists and engineers.

Harlow has an unusual organizational structure. Most companies are organized along functional lines, with separate departments for re-

---

[3]*Houghton* v. *McDonnell Douglas Corporation*, 553 F.2d 561 (C.A. 8 1977).
[4]Abe Fortas, "Age Discrimination in Employment under Federal Law," *Aging and Work* 1, no. 3 (Summer 1978), pp. 147–151.

search and development, engineering, and cost accounting. Harlow is organized around a matrix or task force model. The chief administrative officer, in consultation with department heads, assigns employees from various specialty areas to work on projects. A project team, consisting of computer analysts, engineers, physicists, and support staff, may work together for anywhere from six months to five years. When projects are completed, team members are reassigned to other ongoing projects or await the start-up of new projects.

In recent years, military budget cuts, coupled with the curtailment of several NASA satellite programs, forced Harlow to make a major work force reduction. As projects were completed, many Harlow employees were put on indefinite layoff status. The determination of which employees would be laid off was a point of serious controversy at Harlow. Some employees proposed a seniority system, under which employees with long tenure could exercise the option of selecting reassignment, early retirement, or indefinite layoff status. Employees with little seniority were understandably opposed to this plan.

A second proposal considered by Harlow was that retention be based on individual performance. Under this plan, employees with the best performance records would be retained. Harlow officials argued that the company's matrix organizational design precluded judgments regarding individual performance. Only team performance could be accurately measured, and it was virtually impossible to parcel out individual contributions to a project's success.

After weighing various alternatives, Harlow decided to base retention on each employee's potential contribution to ongoing projects. To implement this plan, the company first assessed human resource needs for all projects funded for at least one more year. One ongoing project, for example, focused on solar energy research. To staff this project, Harlow might retain a relatively new scientist with experience in solar energy conversion, while a more senior scientist with experience in other areas would be placed on indefinite layoff status.

A group of senior scientists who were laid off questioned the work force reduction procedure. They argued that the matching of scientists to projects was arbitrary and subject to bias. They argued further that the company underestimated the ability of senior scientists to contribute to new projects.

Many of the senior staff suspected that they had been laid off, not on the basis of their technical skills, but because they were older and earned among the highest salaries at Harlow. A group of senior researchers retained an attorney who gained access to company records regarding the work force reduction. One document of particular interest to this group showed a breakdown by age and job category of employees who had been retained or laid off (see Table 4–2).

TABLE 4-2

Harlow Industries Work Force Reduction Breakdown: Layoff Percentage by Age and Job Category

Age Category	Physicist	Engineer	Cost Analyst	Computer Programmer	Totals
Under 30 (n = 29)	20	32	35	18	26
31–39 (n = 141)	22	35	36	39	39
40–49 (n = 55)	57	73	81	64	69
50–69 (n = 20)	82	69	78	59	72

The work force reduction data reveal that of 245 professionals employed at Harlow before the layoffs, about 70 percent were under age 40 and about 30 percent were over age 40. Comparison of the layoff percentages across age categories indicates that only slightly more than 30 percent of the employees under age 40 were laid off, while almost 70 percent of the employees over age 40 were laid off. Further analyses confirmed the senior scientists' suspicion that a disproportionate number of older professionals had been laid off indefinitely. But would the statistical evidence be sufficient to prove that Harlow was guilty of age discrimination? The senior scientists decided to press their case.

Discussion of Case 4

Once a prima facie case of age discrimination has been established by the senior scientists, the burden of proof rests with Harlow to demonstrate that its retention decisions were based, not on age, but on the ability of individual scientists to contribute to ongoing projects. In light of Harlow's admitted difficulty in assessing individual contributions to team projects, the company would have to claim that educational background and research experience are valid predictors of a scientist's future contributions. Since older scientists are likely to have a broader range of research experience than younger scientists, Harlow's defense is reduced to justification of retention decisions based on knowledge and education. The company might attempt to show that older scientists suffer from professional obsolescence with respect to Harlow's current research activities. To the extent that the older scientists could refute this allegation, Harlow would be vulnerable to age discrimination charges.

In the past, some organizations have hired scientists and engineers but invested only minimally in their training and development. Many years later, when these scientists and engineers become victims of career obsolescence, the organizations replace them with younger employees who are fully trained in the latest technology. The organizations bear none of the training expense and save further when senior professionals are forced to retire with less than full pension. In the long run, however, an organization's ability to attract and retain professional talent may depend on its reputation for investing in comprehensive career development for its professional staff. Thus organizations with a reputation for ignoring the development needs of senior staff may eventually prove unattractive to young scientists. Moreover, they may be vulnerable to charges of age discrimination on the ground that they deprive senior scientists of training and development opportunities.

The senior scientists' allegation of age discrimination in the Harlow case is supported by statistical evidence. How will the court view this evidence?

Several court decisions in age discrimination cases indicate that statistical evidence relating to a general pattern of age discrimination is properly admitted to support individual discrimination claims. In *Laugesen* v. *Anaconda*, a comparison of average ages of district managers before and after new administrators took over the company was used to support a claim of age discrimination in the discharge of district sales managers.[5]

The case of *Mistretta* v. *Sandia Corporation* is also relevant here.[6] Sandia was found guilty of pervasive age discrimination in termination policies. In 1973, the company instituted a reduction in professional staff affecting about 300 employees. The court decision was strongly influenced by statistical evidence regarding the proportions of younger and older professionals adversely affected by the cutback. Analyses of personnel data indicated that employees between the ages of 55 and 65 made up, by percentage, the smallest age group in the Sandia work force but suffered the greatest impact from the cutback. Apparently without regard to ability or past performance, older employees fared significantly worse than their younger co-workers.

In 1974, Standard Oil of California was involved in a highly publicized age discrimination case over work force reduction policies. During a four-year period, the company had eliminated about 1,600 jobs. Some of the cutback came through normal attrition, but 500 layoffs were necessary. The government charged that 150 of the layoffs, involving senior employ-

---

[5]*Laugesen* v. *Anaconda Co.* (C.A. 6 1975) 9EPP P9870, C10 F.2d 307.
[6]*Mistretta* v. *Sandia Corporation*, 15 FEP Cases 1690 (D. N.M. 1977).

ees, were discriminatory. Standard Oil claimed that the layoffs and discharges had all been necessitated by declining business. The Labor Department countered that the company was attempting to cut costs by firing highly paid older employees and replacing them with younger employees earning lower salaries. The case was resolved when Standard Oil of California awarded $2 million in back pay to 160 employees. Standard Oil agreed to rehire 120 employees and to make back payment awards ranging up to $50,000. The company also reinstated insurance, pension, and stock option benefits to employees.

More recently, Consolidated Edison Company of New York paid $3.7 million in back wages and pension benefits to 156 management employees who had been fired during a reduction in the work force. More than 80 percent of those fired were between the ages of 40 and 65, many of them with performance appraisals in their files indicating "satisfactory" or "excellent" ratings.

In another case, Avco Corporation was found guilty of age discrimination when it failed to recall laid-off older workers, replacing them with younger new recruits.

Layoffs and transfers are not illegal under the ADEA, provided that these actions are based on seniority or performance criteria. The message in recent age discrimination court decisions is that management must be accountable for personnel actions affecting the work status of older employees. Documentation is required to prove that personnel decisions comply with the law. Companies that consistently follow a coherent personnel system, based on reasonable, job-related standards, will certainly be in a much better position to defend their decisions against costly age discrimination suits.

Promotion

In the next case, we illustrate the dilemma that arises when an organization follows inconsistent promotion policies and then tries to justify its decisions.

Case 5: Troublemaker or Age Victim

In 1983 more than 1.2 million workers over age 45 were unemployed. On August 18, 1983, Carleton Jennings, age 63, became one of them. On that day, he was fired from his appliance sales position at Wilsons, a large West Coast department store chain. Here is the chronology of the events that led up to his dismissal.

Between 1976 and 1980, Jennings owned an appliance store in a small northeastern community. Except during the Christmas season, Jennings operated the store by himself—selling appliances, making minor repairs on the appliances he sold, and keeping the books.

During the winter of 1980, Jennings suffered a series of health problems. His doctors advised that he relocate to a warmer climate and take it easy for at least six months. Jennings sold the store and moved to the West Coast. By midsummer, he felt fully recovered, so he decided to return to work. He felt confident that his experience in sales would more than compensate for the fact that he was 59 years old.

Jennings was right. In July 1981, after a brief job search, he found a sales position at Wilsons. He enjoyed working with the other employees in the appliance department and found the job far less taxing than his previous work.

The turnover at Wilsons was quite high, and this was particularly true in the appliance department. In less than two years, Jennings worked under the supervision of three appliance department managers. The first manager was transferred to another store; the second became the manager of a new suburban store; and the third was transferred to the automotive department. In each of these instances, a salesperson from the appliance department or from a related department within the store was promoted to appliance department manager.

In March 1982, Jennings requested that he be considered the next time there was an opening for the appliance department manager's position. He understood that the position required more responsibility than his present position. However, a higher salary, a commission override on appliance sales, and the availability of stock options to department managers made the position financially attractive. Jennings was confident that his experience at Wilsons together with his previous experience in running his own appliance store demonstrated that he was fully qualified for the position.

During the next year, Jennings was passed over for promotion on two occasions. On the first occasion, he expressed his disappointment to Allen Barksdale, the store manager. On the second occasion, he demanded an explanation from the store manager.

On June 9, 1983, Barksdale agreed to meet with Jennings. Barksdale began the interview by reviewing Jennings' work record. Although Wilsons did not have a formal employee review policy, Barksdale referred to handwritten notes from what appeared to be a personnel file. He pointed out that Jennings sales record was only "average." He acknowledged that Jennings was a dependable worker with a good attendance record. He also mentioned that Jennings had made a cash register overring that had cost the department $15. Barksdale concluded that a 63-year-old salesman with an average performance record was not, in his opinion, a top-notch candidate for the department manager's job. Jennings argued that his sales record had consistently exceeded the department quota, that he had once received a commendation for customer courtesy, and that in view of the short tenure of previous department managers his age was not a relevant consideration. The two men debated Jennings' qualifications for another 20 minutes. Barksdale then concluded the meeting and rushed off to another appointment.

During the remainder of the day, Jennings talked about his confrontation with Barksdale to several of his friends in the store. Everyone was sympathetic, and Greta Lewis, who worked in furniture, said it sounded like a case of age discrimination to her. She advised Jennings to talk with a lawyer. Jennings thought the situation over for the next couple of days. Everytime he repeated Barksdale's phrase "not a top-notch candidate," he felt his face redden and his pulse rate rise. Finally, Jennings decided to discuss his case with an attorney.

In retrospect, Jennings realized that he had made a big mistake in discussing his case with other employees. Gossip traveled rapidly at Wilsons. Soon the story spread through the store that Jennings was considering legal action because of his failure to get a promotion.

Between June and August 1983, Carleton Jennings' career and life changed drastically. In June, he received a written warning from the appliance department manager for failing to verify a customer credit voucher. It was common practice for the sales staff to honor such vouchers without verification. As far as Jennings could recall, no one had ever received a written warning for violation of the credit voucher policy.

In July, Jennings was issued a second written warning, this time for extending his afternoon coffee break by five minutes. Jennings refused to sign the warning and wrote his own memo stating that he had skipped his coffee break entirely on numerous occasions when the department had been particularly busy.

Later in July, Jennings' register tally came up $7 short. Jennings could not account for the shortage. Following company policy, the shortage was deducted from his next paycheck.

On August 18, 1983, Jennings was ordered to report to Barksdale's office at the end of the workday. Barksdale informed him that the store periodically monitored customer relations by sending around a "mystery shopper." During the previous week, a mystery shopper had filed a report on his encounter with Jennings. According to the report, Jennings was "abrupt," "impatient," and "not thoroughly knowledgeable about the technical specifications of certain appliances." Barksdale told Jennings that the mystery shopper's report, the two written warnings, the cash register overring, and Jennings' negative attitude toward the store, reflected poorly on the appliance department and on Wilsons' reputation. He said that he had no alternative but to fire Jennings.

Jennings felt sure that Barksdale had decided back in June that Jennings was a "troublemaker" and that the citations and the mystery shopper were Barksdale's ways of demonstrating that Jennings was not only unfit for promotion to department manager, but also unfit to continue working at Wilsons. On the advice of his attorney, Carleton Jennings filed a complaint of employment discrimination with the state Fair Employment Practices Commission. Portions of his complaint are shown in Figure 4–1.

Sixty days after filing his complaint, Jennings received a letter from the Fair Employment Practices Commission indicating that his case had been closed so that he could pursue a court action. Through his attorney, Jennings filed an age discrimination suit in the U.S. district court. Jennings petitioned the court to:

1. Grant a permanent injunction against his employer to prevent the employer from continuing or maintaining policies that limited promotion opportunities for employees in the 40 to 69 age category.
2. Order his employer to institute and carry out equal employment opportunity policies on behalf of persons between the ages of 40 and 69 and to eradicate the effects of the employer's past and present unlawful employment practices.
3. Make appropriate restitution to persons who had been adversely affected by the employer's discriminatory policies and practices, including back pay and other affirmative relief to eradicate the employer's past and present unlawful employment practices, *including* discriminatory promotion policies.
4. Pay attorneys' fees.
5. Grant further relief as the court might deem proper.

Discussion of Case 5

Decisions to terminate older workers are almost always difficult, since managerial motivations for releasing such workers may be subject to different interpretations. Perhaps the best defense against a charge of age bias in a termination decision is the ability to show that the decision was based on the employee's substandard performance or some other legitimate business reason. In cases of substandard performance, managers must be prepared to demonstrate that the employee's behavior was measured fairly and objectively and that the employee was given a reasonable opportunity to bring his performance up to standard. A second consideration in this case is the allegation that once the 63-year-old appliance

FIGURE 4-1

Complaint of Employment Discrimination

TO: Fair Employment Practices Commission

COMPLAINANT'S NAME: Carleton E. Jennings

I WISH TO COMPLAIN AGAINST: Wilsons Department Stores

I BELIEVE THAT I HAVE BEEN DISCRIMINATED AGAINST BECAUSE:

1. I am 63 years old.
2. I was hired as an appliance salesman in April 1980.
3. I believe that my performance on the job was very good.
4. When I was hired, I already had extensive experience in appliance sales and store management. I am sure that I am qualified both for the sales position I held and for promotion to appliance department manager.
5. By practice, qualified sales employees are promoted to managerial positions. I have never been promoted. Younger employees, under 40, have passed over me for promotion to department manager. The most recent opening for which I believe that I should have been promoted occurred during June 1983.
6. I believe that I have been denied access to terms, conditions, wages, and benefits because of my former employer's discriminatory practices and failure to promote me. These include:
   (a) Higher wages.
   (b) Stock options.
   (c) Percentage of commission of departmental sales.
   (d) Retirement benefits.
7. I believe that I have been discriminated against and denied promotion and related terms, conditions, wages, and benefits because of my age.
8. I believe that I was harassed on the job between June and August 1983 and was terminated because I opposed my employer's discriminatory policies.

Carleton E. Jennings

COMPLAINANT'S SIGNATURE

salesman lodged an age discrimination complaint, he was subject to harassment by management.

First, consider the company's promotion policy. It appears that the company follows a policy of promotion from within, under which qualified present employees advance to managerial positions as openings become available. An employee's promotion could be based on sales and managerial experience, educational level, and interpersonal skills or any other combination of job-related criteria. Age should not be a consideration in promotion decisions unless the company can demonstrate that age is a bona fide occupational qualification. In certain unusual circumstances, it might be argued that continuity in office for a minimum of five years is a critical consideration for promotion. Accordingly, candidates for promotion who would reach the company's mandatory retirement age of 70 in less than five years might be rejected. Given the short tenure of most appliance department managers, continuity would not be a valid consideration in this instance.

Next, consider that personnel actions, including both promotion decisions and termination decisions, are more defensible when they are based on a systematic, objective, and job-related performance appraisal system. Moreover, a performance appraisal system that presents employees with periodic feedback on their strengths and weaknesses will help create realistic expectations about promotion opportunities. On the other hand, organizations that fail to develop and administer systematic appraisal and feedback systems are more vulnerable to charges of bias and favoritism. In the appliance department case, the evaluation system is not clear. To the extent that individual evaluations are based on nonsystematic supervisory recommendations, the potential for bias exists.

A final consideration in this case is the allegation that the appliance salesperson's threat to file a complaint regarding age bias in promotion decisions led to managerial harassment, ending in termination. Should this case come to trial, a jury might ultimately decide whether it was merely coincidence that immediately after a protest of age bias in the promotion process, evidence emerged to support the store manager's decision that the complaining employee was neither promotable nor competent to continue in his present position.

Organizational reward systems are often such that it is difficult to own up to mistakes and errors of judgment without risk of negative personal consequences. Numerous examples from business and government can be cited in which individuals have covered up facts, distorted information, and attempted in other ways to justify their errors of judgment. In this context, Barksdale, the store manager, may have been guilty of creating or distorting performance appraisal information, after the fact, to justify dismissing an employee who questioned his judgment. If this proves to be the case, the store manager's actions compound the seriousness of the discriminatory practice. The store manager may be guilty both of practicing age discrimination with respect to promotion practices and of harassing an employee who questioned the legality of these practices.

Should this case go to trial, the outcome is likely to prove costly to Wilsons Department Stores. The calculable costs will include attorneys' fees and the lost time of managers and executives who will have to appear in court. If the case is lost, the restitution of back wages and benefits and the possible reinstatement of the terminated employee will heighten the financial losses.

In addition to the direct costs associated with an age discrimination litigation, there are a number of intangible costs, including the adverse publicity associated with the case and the lowered morale of other older employees. These costs can be significant. Unnecessary costs, both calculable and intangible, resulting from age discrimination litigation can be reduced or eliminated when companies follow well-conceived human resource management policies with respect to the selection, promotion, assessment, and termination of employees.

Avoiding Litigation

The hypothetical cases discussed above illustrate the potential for unconscious age discrimination in a variety of day-to-day managerial decisions. More importantly, they dramatize the importance for managers of becoming thoroughly familiar with the laws regulating the employment of workers in the protected age category 40–69.

Extrapolating from the case examples, managers must be particularly sensitive to decisions that might reflect age considerations in recruiting and selecting employees, recommending employees for training or development opportunities, and promoting employees. In each of these decisions, employee performance or potential, not employee age, should be the governing factor. Similarly, decisions regarding employee transfers, demotions, layoffs, and terminations should be made without regard to age.

Systematic assessment of employee performance on job-related dimensions will provide an important basis for making and defending a range of personnel actions affecting the careers of older workers. Periodic feedback to employees highlighting their strengths and weaknesses and exploring the implications of their present performance for future career moves will help dispel misconceptions and misunderstandings and create realistic expectations about the future. Effective two-way communication between employees and their supervisors at every level in the organization can do much to prevent costly age discrimination litigation.

A key ingredient for avoiding litigation is compliance with both the letter and the spirit of the Age Discrimination in Employment Act. The willingness of management to open-mindedly examine past decisions and correct past errors of judgment with respect to the treatment of older workers will render unnecessary the kind of stonewalling and post hoc justification of poor decisions that was illustrated in Case 5.

Pushing Back Mandatory Retirement

In 1977, amid a storm of controversy, Congress debated the possibility of extending the minimum permissible mandatory retirement age and making several other modifications to the 1967 Age Discrimination in Employment Act.

Arguments in Favor

Those who favored extending the mandatory retirement age beyond 65 argued that forcing retirement at a fixed age represented a blatant form of age discrimination. They felt strongly that an individual's ability to continue working should be assessed on the basis of job-related performance measures, not on the basis of age.

Demographic projections of potential labor shortages brought on by increasing trends toward early retirement coupled with declines in the birthrate were cited as a further reason for permitting employees to work beyond age 65. Also cited were increasing life spans and better health among older people.

Financial considerations were also cited in support of extending the mandatory retirement age. Fears that inflation would erode fixed pension and social security benefits were seen as reversing or at least slowing the trend toward early retirement. Concerns about the solvency of the social security system bolstered the argument that many older workers would desire to continue working full time beyond age 65 or to work on a part-time basis after retirement in order to supplement their postretirement income.

Occupational shifts from heavy manual labor to service, technical, and professional work were seen as enabling older people to remain in the work force longer. Stimulation and psychological fulfillment derived from meaningful work was also mentioned as a reason for allowing employees to continue working beyond age 65.

In summary, those who favored extending mandatory retirement beyond age 65 cited legal, demographic, economic, health, and psychological factors as important considerations for permitting greater individual flexibility in choosing to work or retire.

Management Opposition

Business leaders and college administrators voiced substantial opposition to extending the mandatory retirement age beyond age 65. Lobbyists for business interests argued that the age 65 limit on employment was a fair and equitable policy that minimized favoritism and discrimination. Moreover, corporate executives noted that mandatory retirement at age 65 provided a good opportunity to retire with dignity older workers whose performance levels had dropped badly.

Business leaders also feared that permitting older workers to postpone retirement would clog promotion ladders and reduce opportunities for women, minorities, and younger employees. College administrators echoed this emphasis on "new blood." Managers argued further that human resource plans and labor costs could be estimated with greater certainty under mandatory retirement policies.

Passage of the 1978 Amendments

After weighing the arguments on both sides of the issue, Congress passed the 1978 amendments to the Age Discrimination in Employment Act. The 1978 amendments extended the minimum permissible mandatory retirement age to 70 and abolished mandatory retirement completely for most federal employees. The major features of the amendments are summarized below.

Protection to Age 70.   Prior to the passage of the 1978 amendments, employees could be forced to retire well before age 65 if an earlier retirement date was required by a bona fide company retirement, pension, or benefit plan. This early retirement provision became a point of contention and frequent litigation. Employees forced to retire before age 65 often charged that pension provisions were merely a subterfuge for circumventing the law. The 1978 amendments prohibit the establishment of any retirement, pension, or benefit plan that would require retirement before age 70. Of course, there are no prohibitions against corporate retirement or pension plans that provide financial incentives for voluntary early retirement.

Exceptions.   Exemptions written into the amendments permit mandatory retirement for certain federal positions concerned with public safety. Federal law enforcement officers, fire fighters, pilots, and air traffic controllers, along with employees of the foreign service and the Central Intelligence Agency, are not protected by the amendments.

In the private sector, executives holding high-level policymaking positions who are entitled to an annual pension of at least $27,000 can be retired at age 65. Between 1978 and 1982, tenured university professors could also be terminated at age 65.

Benefit Adjustments.   Employers are allowed to make age-based distinctions in providing benefits for employees who elect to work beyond age 65. An employer need not make contributions to an employee's pension plan after the employee reaches age 65 or make contributions to the pension plan for a newly hired employee who is over age 65.[7] Similarly, employers are not required to actuarially adjust the benefits accrued at the normal retirement age for any employee who continues to work after age 65. In calculating pension benefits, employers need not take into account salary increases awarded after age 65. In other words, employers are not required to make upward adjustments in pension benefits for employees who continue working beyond age 65.

Critics of this concession argue that employers who fail to count years

---

[7]The EEOC is currently developing new rules that will allow older workers to accrue pension benefits for years worked beyond age 65.

worked beyond age 65 in calculating pension benefits create an economic disincentive for extending retirement as permitted under the 1978 amendments. They argue further that business reaps a windfall profit from the concession in two respects. First, by freezing pension contributions, business pays less for older workers. Second, when employees extend their working life, the actual years of pension payout are reduced. Business justifies the freezing of pension contributions as helping to offset the high costs of retaining older workers.

With respect to life insurance and medical benefits, employees in the 65–69 age category are entitled to the same employer contributions as any employee under age 65. Note that because of the increased costs of providing coverage, employer contributions may still result in a percentage reduction in actual coverage for employees over 65.

Effective January 1, 1983, a change in benefit coverage went into effect as part of the Tax Equity and Fiscal Responsibility Act. Employers are now required to include employees between the ages of 65 and 69 in corporate group health plans, unless the employee specifically opts for medicare as his or her primary coverage. While most employees who postpone retirement are expected to elect primary health coverage under their company plan, careful comparison of benefits under both medicare and the company plan will help ensure that each employee elects the most comprehensive coverage available.

Impact of the Amendments

A provision of the 1978 amendments required Department of Labor researchers to study the consequences of extending the mandatory retirement age with an eye to eventually abolishing age-based mandatory retirement altogether. The government report looked at the effects of pushing back the retirement age in the following areas:

Personnel policies, pension and retirement plans.

Career opportunities for younger workers.

Long-term effects of mandatory retirement options.

Estimates of response of older workers to changes in the mandatory retirement age.

Briefly, here is what the Labor Department researchers concluded.[8]

Effects on Personnel Policies, Pension and Retirement Plans.   The most obvious impact of the amendments was to force companies to revise their

---

[8]*Abolishing Mandatory Retirement,* an interim report prepared by the U.S. Department of Labor (Washington, D.C.: U.S. Government Printing Office, 1981).

retirement policies, permitting employees to continue working until age 70. It was widely anticipated that raising the mandatory retirement age would force companies to place greater emphasis on assessing employee performance so as to justify firing poor performers. In fact, three years after the amendments went into effect, no evidence was found that companies were using stricter performance assessment procedures.

With respect to changes in retirement and benefit policies, employers responded by providing more liberal benefits to encourage early or "on-time" retirement. Generous incentives for early retirement included fully accrued pension plans at ages well below 65 and the continuation of company-paid insurance plans after retirement. In the future, when the age of social security eligibility rises to 68, it will be interesting to determine whether corporate pension planners will compensate employees for financial losses in order to encourage retirement at 65. Perhaps the new age for social security eligibility will create a new definition of "on-time" retirement.

Effects on Career Opportunities for Younger Workers, Women, and Minorities. Substantial opposition to extending the retirement age centered on the possibility that retaining older workers would clog promotion channels for younger workers, women, and minorities. Labor Department researchers report that the retention of older workers represents potential competition for only a very small number of younger, female, or black workers (about 4 percent).

Long-Term Effects of the Current Law and Abolition of Mandatory Retirement. Using statistical simulation techniques, Labor Department researchers estimate that under the current age 70 mandatory retirement policy, the labor force participation of men over age 65 will rise by the year 2000 from about 33 percent to 40 percent. This increase nets out to about 217,000 more men over age 65 in the labor force by the year 2000.

Under a policy eliminating mandatory retirement completely, simulations of the participation rates for older workers show a projected addition of 195,000 men over age 70 to the labor force by the year 2000. The predicted total number of male workers who will continue beyond age 65 under complete elimination of mandatory retirement is 412,000, which is an increase of about 10 percent in the labor force participation rate for males in the 60 to 70 bracket. It appears that ending mandatory retirement would permit greater individual flexibility but would have only a minuscule effect on the composition of the total work force.

In summary, research findings suggest that the 1978 amendments provide the option of working beyond age 65 for employees who wish to do so. However, the findings suggest that financial incentives for retiring at or before age 65 exert a strong influence on the retirement intentions and behavior of older employees. Most employees retire at or before age 65, and this trend is likely to continue even though the earliest permissible mandatory retirement age has been pushed up to 70.

Looking Ahead: The End of Mandatory Retirement

There appears to be support from both employees and management for abolishing age-based mandatory retirement policies. A 1981 Harris Poll found that 90 percent of the respondents agreed with this statement: "Nobody should be forced to retire because of age, if he wants to continue working and is still able to do a good job." Respondents in all age categories were equally likely to favor ending mandatory retirement.

There is also some management interest in abolishing mandatory retirement. In a 1981 survey of corporate reactions, 51 percent of employers agreed that "mandatory retirement should be abolished by the end of the decade." Based on projections of potential labor shortages in many occupations, a majority of managers expressed the belief that human resource policies need to be overhauled to encourage older employees to continue working. As of 1982, 38 percent of Fortune 500 companies had thrown out personnel policies calling for mandatory retirement at any age.

One group of business leaders, however, have objected to uncapping retirement policies. Citing the increasing number of age discrimination suits and the growing magnitude of awards to victims of age discrimination, some members of the business community argue that abolishing mandatory retirement would open a Pandora's box of age discrimination litigation. Business lobbyists seem particularly concerned about extending the protection of the ADEA with respect to hiring and promotion discrimination to workers over age 70. Business feels that training costs could not be sufficiently amortized if companies were required to hire employees over age 70.

Legislation abolishing mandatory retirement for all workers has already been enacted by eight states (California, Florida, Iowa, Maine, New Hampshire, Tennessee, Utah, and Vermont). Other states are quite likely to pass similar legislation. Note that the federal ADEA does not preempt state laws that are more liberal with respect to mandatory retirement.

On March 16, 1983, a bill was introduced to further amend the ADEA. The bill calls for abolishing mandatory retirement entirely. Under the proposed amendment, workers over age 40 would be protected from all forms of age discrimination as specified in the ADEA. The end of compulsory retirement is clearly in sight. The implications of this change for corporate personnel policies and management practices are examined in the following chapters.

5

Career Planning
and Management for
Older Employees

Main Issues

- Life-span career planning is becoming more popular.

- Management should link life-span career planning with organizational human resource planning, which in turn must be linked to organizational strategic planning.

- Late career stages and retirement require special planning and flexibility.

In the previous chapter, we tried to help readers become familiar with the various legal requirements governing the employment and retirement of senior employees. We now move beyond the issue of legal compliance to consider the development of age-fair corporate climates that encourage the full utilization of the talents, experience, and dedication of older workers.

By following well-established human resource management practices and considering the special needs of older employees, organizations can do much to promote a corporate value system that respects and supports the contributions of individual employees in every age category. In this chapter, we focus on human resource planning and career management as starting points for helping employees assess their career options within the framework of present and future organizational staffing requirements. The following chapter emphasizes performance review and health assessment systems for early identification of needs for training, transfer, job redesign, or early retirement. In subsequent chapters, we discuss methods to combat employee obsolescence, and we consider innovative flexible retirement options designed to preserve the employability of older workers who wish to postpone their retirement date. Implementation of these human resource management policies should go a long way toward establishing the kind of corporate culture that promotes a sense of security, equity, and commitment.

Managers and administrators who would like to review their own roles and responsibilities in the human resource planning and career management process might ask themselves the following questions:

1. What organizational changes are likely to affect the way my department or unit will operate in the next few years?
2. What changes will take place in the staffing needs of the department in the next few years?
3. Which present employees are likely to need further training or development to remain employable and productive?
4. What are the options for reassigning individuals or redesigning jobs to create a better match between individual skills and abilities and future departmental requirements?
5. In planning for the future, are there any major constraints that must be considered, such as dual-career families, single parents, or employees who would be particularly resistant to relocation?
6. What are the career aspirations and personal development intentions of each employee in the unit or department? Are individual career plans realistic, given organizational strategic plans?
7. What are the retirement intentions of each employee in the unit? Do any employees plan to postpone their retirement?
8. How important is it to organizational effectiveness, to my own managerial effectiveness, and to the security, motivation, and career advancement of each of my employees for me to answer these questions knowledgeably? Do I need to give human resource management and career planning a higher priority among my future managerial activities?

In our experience, human resource management and career planning have not been high-priority managerial responsibilities until very recently. Yet the payoffs for a comprehensive effort to manage human resources effectively are great for the organization, for managers, and for individual employees.

Underutilization of human resources occurs when individuals find themselves in career ruts and dead-end jobs or with obsolete skills. The result is often low motivation and marginal performance. Managers would not invest capital at a 4 percent rate of return if investment opportunities with identical risk levels offer a 10 percent return. Similarly, to be competitive, management must strive to maximize rates of return through the full utilization of human assets.

In this chapter, we will consider the steps necessary for integrating corporate human resource plans with individual career goals. We focus special attention on the career planning issues that are important to the full utilization of older employees.

We begin with a brief examination of recent changes in the nature of work and the implications of these changes for human resource planning and career management. Our analysis suggests that technological changes will create new opportunities for persons trained in the scientific and technical fields, but at the cost of displacing production, staff, and middle-management personnel and at the risk of rapidly accelerating the potential obsolescence of many older workers.

We show how comprehensive human resource plans coupled with career counseling will help managers determine effective responses to shifting organizational priorities and human resource needs. We review the key elements in an effective human resource plan, emphasizing particularly the payoffs for maintaining the productive employment of older workers.

Next we focus on the development of career management systems. Corporate responsibilities for establishing both formal and informal programs for lifetime career management systems are reviewed. We conclude that the ultimate responsibility for career management rests with the individual employee. Employees who fail to recognize this responsibility risk potential obsolescence and mid-career or late career crises.

Increased Importance of Human Resource Planning

In the opening chapter, we traced the revolutionary changes that have been sweeping across U.S. industry. Economic, technological, and legal forces have unalterably changed the complexion of American business. Foreign competition and soaring interest rates during the period of 1979–83 forced plant closings and high unemployment in such diverse industries as steel, apparel, construction, and automobiles. At the same time, a boom in high-technology specialities, including computer software, biomedical engineering, telecommunications, robotics, fiber optics, and laser applications, created new employment opportunities for persons with advanced training. During this transition period, millions of production workers were laid off, with bleak prospects for future employment. Unemployment reached up into the managerial ranks and even into the executive suites as cost-conscious companies pared down staff positions.

Even as the economy improves, companies are moving very slowly with respect to restaffing. Some companies have moved away from their formerly paternalistic philosophy of providing job security for loyal, longtime employees and are now adopting a leaner, more competitive philosophy demanding higher performance and greater quality from a slimmed-down work force. Other companies have permanently sliced off layers of staff and middle-level managers in favor of more decentralized and integrated organizational structures. Still other companies are systematically replacing several generations of production workers whose skills have grown obsolete with robots and with technicians to keep the robots oiled and running smoothly.

When women, minorities, and younger workers compete with older workers who exercise their legal options to postpone retirement beyond age 65, managers will have to walk a tightrope to ensure fair and equitable treatment to all segments of the labor force. Decisions made today will have significant morale and career consequences for those who continue working, economic and psychological consequences for those who are displaced, and potential legal consequences for the decision makers.

Starting with Corporate Strategic Plans

Human resource planning is the process of estimating future personnel needs and developing plans to ensure that those needs will be met. Human resource plans must be integrated with corporate strategic plans. The implementation of corporate strategic plans depends on the close coordination of those plans with human resource plans whether the strategic plans call for expansion or contraction; merger, acquisition, or divestment; the introduction of new products and services; the development of new production technologies; or the abandonment of obsolete manufacturing processes. Consider the following example.

Case 1:   Technological Change

The strategic plans of a manufacturer of budget-priced men's ready-to-wear clothing call for the introduction within three years of a new line of custom-made suits and sports coats. As a result of a recent breakthrough in computer graphics, company executives predict that it will be possible to custom-make clothing at a relatively low cost. Implementation of this revolutionary new manufacturing technology, however, will require significant changes in the mix of production, marketing, sales, and managerial skills throughout the company. The technology will be "on-line" in a little over two years.

The challenge of ensuring that trained employees will be in place to implement the strategic plan by the target date falls on the shoulders of division managers and human resource planners. Whether the human resource plans fit in with the strategic plans depends on how well managers

Trends in Labor Force Participation of Older People by Sex, 1950–1980

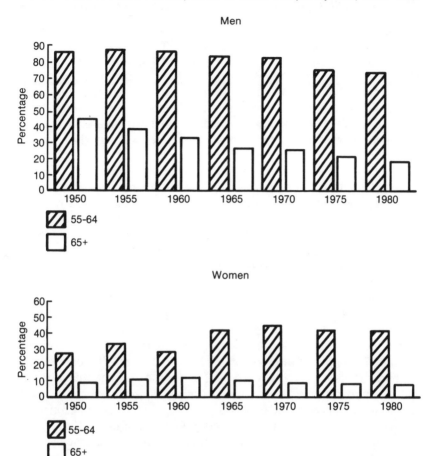

Source: U.S. Department of Labor *Employment and Training Report of the President* (Washington, D.C.: U.S. Government Printing Office, 1982).

and planners mesh individual career goals, aptitudes, and potential with future organizational staffing needs.

When corporate changes affect the career paths of senior employees, managers must be particularly sensitive to potential fears and insecurities created among older workers. Often concerns over job security can be overcome by effective planning and systematic retraining efforts, as illustrated in the following case.

Case 2: Cutback: Retraining and Retaining

A major engine manufacturer with facilities throughout the Midwest projected a significant drop in demand both for large engines used in farm machinery and for smaller engines used in appliances and hand tools. Part of the projected drop in business could be attributed to an economic slowdown and part to lower prices offered by foreign competitors. Corporate strategic planners concluded that in order to remain competitive, the company should close down several of its oldest and least efficient manufacturing facilities. In addition, the planners considered it imperative that more efficient production methods and quality control measures be instituted immediately.

With respect to its manufacturing plant in Allentown, Pennsylvania, the company planned to increase the number of robots used in the assembly process by more than 40 percent over a three-year period, displacing low-skilled and semiskilled production workers with a smaller number of technicians and robotics troubleshooters.

A comprehensive three-year human resource management plan was developed. First, a complete hiring freeze for production workers went into effect. The planners projected that through retirements and natural attrition, an 18 percent drop in production workers would occur in the next three years. Second, the planners worked with benefit specialists to provide new incentives for early retirement. It was expected that another 7 percent of the production work force would be both eligible for and interested in early retirement under the new financial arrangements. Third, foremen, shop supervisors, and line managers worked together to identify qualified employees who would be interested in entering a three-year company-sponsored training program in robotics. The goal here was to retrain a sufficient number of current employees to staff and maintain the automated production facility. Plans were also made to offer transfers to displaced workers, either to other departments within the plant or to plants in other parts of the country. The company's goal was to lay off or terminate as few employees as possible.

Ted Englehardt had worked in the Allentown plant as a machinist for over 23 years. Although lacking much in the way of a formal education, Ted had worked his way up to a $22,000-a-year job. He lived in a comfortable suburban apartment, drove a Camaro, and had a small nest egg to help his daughter with college tuition. Understandably, Ted was stunned when rumors spread through the plant last winter that a major reorganization was under consideration, including the possibility of closing several production lines.

Ted immediately considered the options available to him if he were laid off or terminated. At 48, he was understandably concerned about competing with recent high school and college graduates for entry-level positions in other companies. He also felt that at this stage in his life, particularly with his limited educational background, returning to school or entering a vocational program might pose some real problems, including financial hardships. With high unemployment throughout the area, Ted nervously contemplated the prospects of uprooting his family and traveling to the Sunbelt in search of work.

During the next two months, Ted had several meetings with his supervisor and the plant's industrial relations representative. Ted agreed to take several aptitude tests and was later offered the opportunity to attend the robotics training program. Although this meant attending classes at 6:45 A.M., working his regular shift, and then studying late into the evening, Ted felt that the retraining program offered him an opportunity for more job security and for advancement into what he called a "more professional" job.

Effective human resource planning in this instance provided sufficient time for retraining a long-tenured employee so that he could contribute to the company's evolving corporate needs. The company's investment in retraining was substantial, as were the sacrifices made by Ted Englehardt to complete the program. Note, however, that the benefits were also substantial. From the company's perspective, a hardworking employee with a 23-year-record of good performance and loyalty was retained. Recruiting, selection, and orientation costs associated with hiring a new employee were saved. Moreover, it is reasonable to assume that, given his new security within the plant, Ted Englehardt will develop an even higher level of commitment and loyalty in future years.

From Ted Englehardt's perspective, the opportunity to continue with the company and to advance into more complex and responsible positions was attractive. Also important to Ted was avoiding the personal, family, and financial costs of job loss.

Finally, the societal benefits were significant. The tangible savings included the expenses associated with unemployment compensation, possible welfare subsidies, and other family services. As a gainfully employed worker, Ted Englehardt paid federal and state taxes and contributed to social security. The intangible savings may have included a reduction of the social costs that accompany the mental and physical problems associated with long-term unemployment.

Companies interested in preserving and protecting the jobs of senior employees can benefit greatly from developing comprehensive human resource plans and encouraging employees at every age to develop individual career plans. Accordingly, we now turn to a systematic look at the entire human resource planning and career management process.

Predicting Human Resource Needs

Figure 5-1 illustrates the entire human resource planning process. Note that once strategic plans have been formulated, management must forecast the implications of these long-range plans for the makeup of the work force several years into the future. In our ready-to-wear clothing example, managers and planners might anticipate the need for employees with computer graphic skills, for fabric cutters with special experience in working from computer-generated patterns, and for additional salespersons. At the same time, production managers might estimate that fewer produc-

---

FIGURE 5-1

The Human Resource Planning Process

Starting with corporate strategic plans
(expand/contract; acquire/diversify/merge/divest;
new product/new market/new service)

↓

Predicting future human resource needs
(mix of skills, training, experience/age, sex, race needed to
fulfill strategic plans)

↓

Assessing current internal human resources
(characteristics and demographics of current work force,
including past performance, potential, health, career
aspirations, interests and experiences, education, and
training)

↓

Assessing external human resources
(demographic, economic, legal, social, labor market)

↓

Deriving a human resource strategy
(dealing with oversupply, maintaining steady state, responding
to shortages)

↓

Implementing human resource planning
(recruitment, selection, training, motivation, compensation,
transfer, retirement, termination)

↓

*Integrating corporate strategic plans with individual career
plans*

---

tion workers, sewers, tailors, and inventory specialists will be needed in the future.

Although predicting work force requirements is an inexact process, several techniques can be utilized for this purpose, including the "expert estimate" technique, the trend projection technique, simulation modeling, and the unit demand forecasting technique. Numerous books and articles give the details of these techniques.

Will the company find qualified employees within its current work force to staff the anticipated new positions? And what will become of the employees whose jobs will be eliminated? In order to answer these important questions, management must be thoroughly familiar with the characteristics and aspirations of current employees.

Assessing Current Internal Human Resources

Once organizational mid-range and long-range objectives have been set and strategic plans formulated, human resource planners and line managers face the difficult task of projecting the kinds of skills, education, training, and experience that employees will need in order to meet future organizational requirements. The next logical step in formulating a comprehensive human resource plan is to conduct a thorough inventory of the current work force. This inventory, sometimes referred to as a human resource analysis, includes a tabulation of the numbers of workers in various units, departments, sections, and divisions of the organization; a profile of each employee's skill level; information about present and past performance levels; estimates of future potential; salary histories; career aspirations; and personal characteristics such as race, sex, and age.

Larger organizations have computerized human resource inventories. Elaborate systems of cross-referencing allow planners to identify almost instantly the individuals with special skills who are available to take on new assignments. For example, a large petroleum refiner could quickly identify the French-speaking geologists with at least two years of oceanographic experience, who were available and willing to accept a temporary assignment to work on a joint venture with a foreign subsidiary.

Note that the effectiveness of a human resource inventory depends on managerial efforts to maintain and update information concerning each individual working under their supervision. To keep individual files up to date, performance reviews must be current, special training programs and unique work experiences must be recorded, and changing career aspirations must be noted.

To keep abreast of employees' career aspirations, managers must find opportunities to chat with employees about their career goals. It is particularly important for managers to be alert to employees in mid-career who have reached a plateau in their current career path and may need a change. Similarly, frank discussions with older workers regarding their current retirement intentions, their desires for reduced work schedules, or their interest in possible new roles in late career stages provide important inputs to a human resource inventory.

To ensure the accuracy of inventory data, a few companies have invited employees to review their own files periodically; to challenge entries that are not reflective of their performance, potential, or aspirations; and to make revisions where necessary.

As shown in Figure 5-1 in addition to developing an accurate picture of the present work force, managers and human resource planners need to follow environmental trends that could affect the supply and demand of potential employees with various combinations of skills and training.

Assessing External Resources

Effective human resource planning requires consideration of the environmental opportunities and constraints that are likely to influence the recruitment, selection, training, and retention of employees with the proper mix of skills and experience to meet future job demands. In recent years, a number of environmental factors, including demographic, economic, legal, and social factors, have had a profound influence on human resource planning.

Demographic Trends

Demographers project an aging work force. The median age of the U.S. workforce fell to a low of 34.8 in 1982. However, the median age is projected to rise to 37.3 by 1995. Demographers predict that the transition will be far from smooth. The changing demographics of the work force will create shortages among workers in some age categories as well as career gridlocks for baby boomers competing among themselves for a limited number of advancement opportunities.

From present demographic and retirement trends, a serious shortage of experienced senior managers and executives can be extrapolated for the years 1985–90. And, according to one management consultant, "It is astounding how few corporations recognize the shortfall." Companies looking for experienced leaders to guide new ventures and supervise the large number of 20- to 34-year-olds who will enter the job market in coming years may find themselves with too many empty desks in their executive suites. One obvious solution, of course, would be to implement policies

Median Age of the Labor Force

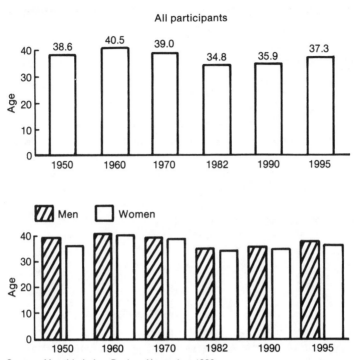

Source: *Monthly Labor Review*, November 1983.

aimed at encouraging older managers to postpone their retirement. Another would be to identify the most talented younger managers and "fast-track" them up the corporate ladder. Clearly, effective human resource planning requires careful consideration of demographic trends.

Economic Trends

Planners also need to follow economic cycles. Past experience has shown that significant costs are associated with work force fluctuations resulting from changes in the economy. These costs include the costs of recruiting and training workers during expansionary periods as well as the costs of unemployment compensation during recessionary periods. Moreover, there are intangible costs, including the diminished loyalty and commitment of an insecure work force. In order to avoid the personal and corporate hardships inflicted by layoffs and plant closings during tough economic times, planners are considering various strategies that are designed to buffer the work force against sudden downturns in the economy.

In order to offset the problems of work force instability, corporations such as Control Data, IBM, and Delta Air Lines have adopted policies of guaranteed employment. Control Data, for example, uses part-time employees, overtime, and subcontracting as ways to avoid overhiring during peak periods followed by mass layoffs during business slowdowns. IBM has been able to adhere to a 35-year-old policy of no layoffs. Through a program of retraining, IBM employees develop a range of skills that permits flexibility for reassignments as dictated by corporate needs. Other companies have used temporary employees during busy times to maintain work force stability. A major insurance company, for example, has created its own temporary help pool from retired workers interested in continuing with the company on a reduced work schedule. Long-term human resource plans require a special sensitivity to changing economic conditions and creative approaches to avoid sharp fluctuations in work force requirements.

Legal Trends

Human resource planners must keep abreast of changes in employment laws. For example, the abolition of mandatory retirement at a fixed age combined with new social security incentives to continue working could encourage more older workers at every level in the organization to postpone their retirement. Yet plans to encourage older workers to continue working have been strongly criticized on the grounds that they increase the burden on organizations to evaluate older workers for continued employment, that they increase the costs associated with the retention of high-salaried older employees, and that they block promotion opportunities for women and minorities. The blocking of promotion opportunities may be particularly problematic in organizations that have come under pressure to reach specific affirmative action objectives. Legislative changes mandating new personnel policies governing women, minorities, handicapped workers, and older employees as well as changes in the regulations governing compensation, pensions, and benefits must be carefully monitored by human resource planners in order to ensure that long-range work force plans are compatible with government regulations.

Social Value Trends

Changing social values represent another external factor influencing corporate human resource planning. In recent years, the entry into the work force of increasing numbers of career-oriented women and dual-career families has dramatically influenced a broad range of organizational policies governing everything from mobility patterns to fringe benefits. In addition, a better-educated work force has demanded more meaningful and challenging jobs. Interest in self-actualization often translates into demands for more vacation time to pursue outside activities, and changing patterns of work and leisure have led to a consistent trend toward retirement at a younger age. Human resource plans should anticipate how changing social values will influence the career goals and aspirations of employees in the future.

Occupational Trends

Planners must also monitor the numbers of individuals who are currently preparing for various occupations and the likely demand for specialists in various occupational categories. During the past decade, we have witnessed a shortage of nurses, accountants, and computer programmers. At the same time, an oversupply of teachers, attorneys, and dentists has created frustrations for many who have been unable to find employment compatible with their formal training.

Often environmental factors work in combination to create labor shortages or gluts. For example, a Food and Drug Administration regulation requiring more comprehensive testing of new drugs on laboratory animals creates an instant need for animal pathologists within the pharmaceutical industry. On the other hand, technological advances in solar energy combined with tighter government control over offshore oil drilling could restrict career opportunities for petroleum geologists.

In order to better prepare themselves for demographic, economic, legal, social, and labor market trends, human resource planners have adopted a number of forecasting techniques. They have complemented their statistical projections with the Delphi method for speculating about future events. This method taps the insights of experts in the areas of social, economic, and technological change. Independently generated scenarios about future events are developed by each expert. The experts' projections are collected, reviewed, and refined. Then the results are returned to the experts so that they can rank the likelihood that each of the various scenarios will occur. The goal is to spot trends and identify potential obstacles that must be overcome in order to carry out plans for the future.

Deriving a Human Resource Strategy

Referring again to Figure 5-1, note that predictions of future staffing requirements are based in part on corporate strategic plans. Estimates of future needs must also take into account the normal flow of workers through the organization. Based on historical patterns of movement, planners can develop transition charts showing the probability that employees in each organizational position will remain in the organization, transfer laterally, advance, or leave the organization.

Armed with information about future staffing demands based on estimates derived from strategic plans, managers can examine the inventory of the present work force and assess how well future needs can be met by using existing internal and external resources and existing personnel policies. When organizational goals and corporate strategies remain unchanged, it may be quite likely that future staffing needs will be satisfied without major revisions of corporate personnel policies. On the other hand, when corporate goals require the organization to move in new directions, perhaps adopting new technologies, providing new products and services, divesting some operations, and acquiring others, it is likely that special policies and procedures will be needed to assure the right mix of human resources. Frequently, demands for new skills and talents are created in some job categories, while oversupplies of workers are identified in other categories. In these instances, managers and planners must work together to identify what role each employee will play in the future. Managers and planners must also collaborate in determining what changes in personnel policies are necessary in order to ensure that the human resources required to carry out organizational strategic plans are in place.

Implementation of Human Resource Planning: Basic Considerations

Implementation of an effective human resource plan frequently requires adjustment of existing personnel policies. For example, when it has been determined that some future needs can be fulfilled only from external sources, programs of recruitment and selection must be developed. In some instances, recruiters might be dispatched to college campuses, to technical schools, or to scientific conferences in order to identify a pool of applicants with the necessary qualifications. When a proven track record of managerial experience is required, companies may retain the services of executive search firms to help identify experienced managers interested in new career opportunities.

Many planners have learned from their own past experience that individuals with special skills and unique talents are likely to be in short supply. This can result in bidding wars, as so often happens in professional sports. To avoid this, companies must develop systematic ongoing programs of recruitment and selection. It is not unusual for corporate recruiters to work closely with university guidance counselors and placement officials to encourage students to major in future "high demand" areas, such as computer technology or medical engineering.

Perhaps the biggest challenge for human resource planners is to develop strategies to ensure that present employees match well with future organizational staffing requirements. Personnel programs specifying annual reviews of performance and potential may need to be upgraded. Compensation and benefit programs may need to be revised in order to retain and motivate present employees. Training and development programs are often instituted to maintain productivity, overcome obsolescence, and groom future corporate leaders. Promotion, transfer, and relocation programs may be revised.

The development of employee progression charts, particularly at managerial levels, helps management identify employees who are ready for promotion now or in the near future. Progression charts have proven especially useful for developing individual career plans for fast-track employees. The progression chart helps both managers and employees develop realistic plans regarding the optimal mix of training and experience necessary for career advancement.

Finally, retirement policies may be reexamined either to hasten the retirement of workers whose skills no longer fit corporate needs or to encourage postponed retirement for workers whose skills and experience may be particularly important to meeting future organizational objectives.

Computer simulation or "what if" models can be used to determine in a probabilistic way the implications of various personnel policies for staffing levels. For example, managers can model the likely effects of a new job rotation and promotion plan on meeting affirmative action targets. They can model the effects of added financial incentives for early retirement or added inducements for postponed retirement on the age distribution of workers in various job categories. Simulations also provide planners with cost estimates of various personnel strategies. By comparing salary and benefits costs along with the program costs associated with alternative personnel actions, managers can make more informed decisions about the kinds of personnel policy revisions that will prove most cost effective.

Integrating with Individual Career Plans

Referring once again to Figure 5-1: the final step in a comprehensive human resource plan requires close integration of projections of organizational staffing needs with individual career aspirations. In recent years, a growing number of companies have recognized that corporate-wide career management programs can pay dividends in employee commitment and productivity. Accordingly, companies are experimenting with innovative career management approaches, including multiple career paths, on-the-job development opportunities, career planning workshops, individual career counseling, and mentor-protégé relationships. A few companies have learned through bitter experience that poorly conceived career management programs risk creating a cycle of unrealistically raised employee expectations, disappointment, reduced commitment, and organizational disruption. On the other hand, a career management program that carefully integrates human resource plans, performance and potential assessments, and training and development activities with individual planning can lead to bottom line improvements in employee retention, flexibility, commitment, and productivity.

The actual implementation of a career management program takes many forms. In some companies, the creation of career information centers provides a mechanism for alerting employees to the position vacancies and training and development activities that are available throughout the company. In addition, posting job vacancies gives employees first priority to bid on transfers and promotions and helps stimulate career advancement. A more sophisticated approach to career planning involves grouping jobs into job families within and across departmental lines. Job families, groups of jobs with similar requirements, help identify positions throughout the organization that employees might qualify for based on their present experience. They also help career counselors and employees plan career paths tailored to individual skills and aspirations.

The importance of top-level support and commitment for a career management program cannot be stressed enough. With support from the top, the message comes through loud and clear at all organizational levels that career planning and development are a key part of every manager's job.

Managers must work closely with human resource planners to identify employees who are good candidates to fill key future organizational roles. High-potential employees then have sufficient time to prepare for new career paths and for advancement through formal training and special broadening work assignments. At Union Carbide, for example, rotation of job assignments provides middle-level managers with exposure to many parts of the organization. At other companies, appointment to company-wide management committees or special executive task forces provides managers targeted for increased responsibilities with a top-down perspective on the company. Experience gained as a special staff assistant to a top-level executive represents still another way of getting the "big picture" perspective necessary for career advancement. Many companies develop intricate plans for coupling advanced management education with challenging job assignments to prepare individual managers for future corporate roles.

Career planning is not limited to the managerial ranks. Another critical dimension of career management involves scientific and technical personnel. Here the focus is both on avoiding the dangers of technical obsolescence and on proactive planning of career advancement opportunities. For some organizations, combating technological obsolescence takes the form of in-service training, opportunities to attend update programs and professional meetings, and even paid sabbaticals to keep abreast of recent innovations, theories, and applications. Of equal importance, scientific and technical personnel often face conflicting pressures to choose between remaining in their area of technical expertise and pursuing advancement through the managerial ranks. With the help of professional career counselors, scientific and technical employees are better able to keep their skills current and to make difficult choices regarding future career paths.

Often stimulated by affirmative action pressures, corporate planners have also been concerned with career management programs at lower levels within the organization. In some instances, efforts have been made to encourage women to move into traditionally male occupations. In other instances, male employees have requested job assignments to what have traditionally been female occupations. Beyond affirmative action considerations, career counselors can help clerical and production employees consider the kinds of training and experience necessary for advancement up the corporate hierarchy.

During periods of rapid technological change, perhaps the most important function of career management programs is to identify job categories where future corporate needs are likely to be low and to help employees in these categories to chart a new career course. Preparing employees to move into high-demand career tracks compatible with their interests, skills, and aspirations represents a true integration of human resource planning and career management.

While formal organization-wide programs to encourage career planning heighten awareness of occupational information and new career paths, the day-to-day sharing of information between managers and employees provides an invaluable source of career guidance and counseling on a continuing basis. In some cases, managers serve as information conduits, alerting employees to upcoming changes that could have important career implications. In other cases, managers serve as a sounding board, allowing employees to express aspirations, plans, and intentions and to obtain honest feedback about the likelihood of achieving their career goals. In still other cases, managers may intervene directly to help employees obtain needed training or cope with stress and burnout or to redesign job requirements so as to help employees get back on track.

Given the importance of these added responsibilities to serve as career counselors and critical links between organizational long-range human resource plans and individual career aspirations, managers should be given appropriate help. Here are several ways to increase managerial effectiveness in the area of career guidance:

1. Managers should be informed, well in advance, of changes that could alter the mix of skills and experience necessary to fulfill job requirements in their units or departments.
2. Managers should be provided with information about seminars, workshops, and training programs offered both within and outside the company that their employees are eligible to attend.
3. Managers should be encouraged to learn more about key career issues, including managing the plateaued employee, diagnosing and coping with career burnout, and redesigning jobs to maximize employee contributions.
4. Managers should be kept informed of corporate policies with respect to retirement options, including possibilities for part-time employment, job sharing, phaseout programs, temporary postretirement work opportunities, and consulting arrangements.
5. Managers should be encouraged to attend workshops designed to enhance coaching and counseling skills, including listening, goal setting, problem solving, and career path planning.

In order to encourage systematic managerial attention to the important issues surrounding career planning, top management needs to recognize, support, and reward those administrators and managers who conscientiously make career planning a high-priority activity.

Special Approaches for Mid-Career and Older Employees

Clearly, long-range planning efforts can benefit employees of all ages. When planning takes into account the special needs of older workers, benefits accrue to the individual employee, the corporation, and society.

Figure 5–2 shows a model of the stages in career development. Of particular concern is the period around age 40. According to career researchers, this marks an important juncture, leading to growth and development for some, a career plateau for others, and the onset of career stagnation for still others.

Managers must recognize that mid-career choices are made in the larger context of life events. As they approach their 40s, individuals start to develop a fuller appreciation for their advancing age. Often body changes associated with aging lead to a new appreciation for the limits of mortality. Individual reactions to these insights vary greatly, as shown in Figure 5–2. For some, this mid-life period leads to a search for new goals and challenges and a determination to continue working toward unmet career

FIGURE 5-2

Stages in Career Development

Stages in career development

Source: Adapted from Donald E. Super and Douglas T. Hall, "Career Development: Exploration and Planning," *Annual Review of Psychology* 29 (1978), p. 351.

aspirations. For others, mid-life becomes a period of reflection and questioning about whether goals are realistic, whether dreams will be realized, and whether work-related sacrifices are worth the price. When the answers are positive, individuals may move into a period of security, dedication, and equilibrium. On the other hand, when dissatisfaction over unfulfilled goals develops, individuals often lose motivation and energy. For these individuals, the transition period, referred to as a mid-life crisis, frequently leads to disruptive family relationships and career switches, and mid-career marks the beginning of inadequacy and insecurity feelings, concerns about obsolescence, decreased mobility, job insecurity, and subsequent career stagnation.

Managers should provide the support and guidance necessary to help individuals through the difficult mid-career stage. As we have noted, the creative corporate responses to career crisis include professional counseling, opportunities for job rotation, sabbaticals and new opportunities for training, development, and challenge.

Returning to Figure 5-2, the period beginning at about age 65 marks a potential point of career decline. At this traditional age of retirement, according to the model, individuals come to terms with their accomplishments and begin to shift their attention to nonwork activities. However, we know from our previous discussion of individual differences that individual variability is great among older workers. While some senior workers have started to prepare for retirement much earlier in their careers, others have made the decision to continue working as long as possible. Corporate efforts to provide preretirement counseling permit individuals to think through their retirement plans in light of their financial, health, family, and job requirements.

Individual Responsibilities for Self-Management

In the "Cutback: Retraining and Retaining" case earlier in this chapter, Ted Englehardt and his fellow trainees in the robotics program were lucky to be employed by a company that followed forward-thinking human resource management practices. Not all employees benefit from comprehensive corporate efforts to retain and retrain longtime workers. Consider the fate of Robert Blackburn, a 56-year-old regional marketing manager.

Case 3:   Too Young to Retire, Too Old to Manage

Robert Blackburn worked for a Minnesota-based manufacturer of frozen and packaged foods. For five years, he had supervised a sales staff of 25 charged with the responsibility of negotiating supermarket shelf and freezer space for the company's products. At $60,000 a year in salary, plus benefits, perks, and stock options, he fulfilled the role of a successful manager. In fact, he felt confident that he was a serious contender for the national marketing manager's position.

About three years ago, corporate realignments led to the development of a more decentralized marketing structure and ultimately to the elimination of five regional marketing manager positions, including Blackburn's. Twenty weeks' severance pay and an option to elect early retirement at greatly reduced pension benefits were all that the company offered Blackburn.

As with so many other middle managers caught in corporate reorganizations, Blackburn's initial reactions were shock and disbelief. While he could understand the company's motivation for reorganization, he found it difficult to accept the fact that so little effort was made to help him carve out a new role in another corporate division. His initial impulse was to retain counsel and bring suit against the company for employment discrimination.

According to Blackburn, the first six months of unemployment were filled with frustration and feelings of rejection. During this period, Blackburn sent out over 300 résumés and contracted for the services of two executive placement services. These efforts netted him less than a dozen job interviews and not a single offer.

His wife, Joanne Blackburn, returned to work as an administrative assistant for a real estate firm. Her $15,000 annual salary along with modest quarterly dividends from their investments represented the family's only sources of income.

Some nine months after his separation, Robert and Joanne Blackburn reassessed their future. Too young to retire, yet apparently too old to land a managerial position in marketing, Blackburn searched for other career options. If the economy improved, he could continue his job search. Or he could lower his career aspirations and apply for nonmanagerial sales positions. Lowering career aspirations, the Blackburns recognized, meant a commitment to living permanently on a substantially lower income. A third alternative considered by the Blackburns involved starting their own small business. At first, a small business venture seemed the most difficult and risky option.

Although Blackburn had read about others who had parlayed hobbies and outside interests into small businesses, he had no desire for such a radical career shift. After carefully evaluating his own skills and experience, he concluded that his comparative advantage in the business world centered on his marketing knowledge and experience. Capitalizing on his background, at age 57 and almost one year after his termination, Blackburn decided to start his own marketing and sales consulting business.

Blackburn operated Blackburn and Associates, Consultants, out of his attic loft. Starting with a business card, stationery, and a list of local retailers, the former marketing manager went to work selling himself and his new venture.

A small stereo retailer became his first client. Several months later, a hardware chain with 15 outlets contracted for marketing consultation. By the end of the first year, Blackburn had developed a list of seven new clients and earned over $28,000. Although he now worked longer hours for much less pay, he viewed his situation as a beginning on a second career. He loved working for himself, looked forward to the future optimistically, and felt at age 57 that his life was again on track.

Robert Blackburn and a great many individuals of all ages are starting to recognize that careers must be managed. Given the rapidly changing corporate environment, individuals can no longer afford the luxury of watching passively as their careers unfold. Rather, they have come to appreciate that they must assume responsibility for managing their own careers and that career planning must be a continuous process spanning the full range of stages from first-job selection to retirement preparation.

For individuals who might be in situations like Robert Blackburn's, the time to start is immediately. Individual career planning begins with a critical self-analysis of interests, skills, and potential. Then short- and longer-term career goals are formulated. The goals ought to be specific and in writing. Written plans should include a game plan for capitalizing on strengths and overcoming obstacles to career aspirations. Written timetables help individual career planners assess their progress along the way.

Of particular importance to mid-career and older individuals is the development of contingency plans in the event that their careers get unexpectedly sidetracked. Security often breeds complacency with regard to contingency career planning. What are the options for senior employees when their careers become derailed? One obvious option is to search for a new employer. As illustrated in the Blackburn case, competition is keen and older managers are often seen as too expensive compared to younger applicants. Those older managers lucky enough to receive job offers need to go beyond consideration of salary, incentives, and perks in evaluating new opportunities; they must also examine the prospective employer's reputation and financial standing. Companies in financial trouble or ripe for takeovers have been known to entice experienced managers with lucrative offers when long-run career prospects may be very uncertain.

Changing careers is certainly much riskier and often much more traumatic than merely changing employers. However, when professionals face long-term unemployment or come up against limited growth opportunities in their present positions, a career switch may prove worth the risk. Again, an honest self-assessment of marketable skills can be an important first step in preparing for a career change. Batteries of interest inventories, aptitude tests, and career information booklets are available to help identify new career tracks where skills are immediately transferable.

Launching a new career often involves the financial sacrifices associated with accepting entry-level positions. For many career changers, however, the excitement, challenge, and growth opportunities in second careers offset short-run monetary sacrifices.

Not all of the second careers of senior employees are consequences of stumbling blocks in their career paths. To the contrary, a sizable number of managers, scientists, and professionals in the 35–50 age range are consciously dropping out of the corporate marathon. Some are motivated by changing values, mid-life reassessments of goals, newly acquired interests, and the desire to pursue secret lifetime ambitions. Others have recognized the early symptoms of career burnout, in which fatigue and frustration replace enthusiasm and creativity. Still others pursue a second career in conjunction with early retirement. Regardless of the motivation, those about to start on second careers should be forewarned that a lack of instant success in their new endeavors can result in a loss of confidence and a big letdown. Experts claim that family support during the transition period between careers is particularly helpful.

Effective career management requires individual responsibility for setting goals, periodically assessing progress, and developing contingency options. At each stage of the game from selecting the first job to embarking on a postretirement second career, the need for active management is critical. As in other areas of business, effective management requires careful planning, systematic evaluation of options, execution of strategic plans, and flexibility in responding to the unexpected. Had Robert Blackburn been an active career manager, he might have saved himself a year of uncertainty and frustration.

Summary

Human resource management and career planning are a joint responsibility of corporate and personnel planners, line managers and administrators, and each individual employee. In many instances, integrating long-term human resource plans with individual career aspirations rests with line managers and administrators at every organizational level. In order to fulfill this important responsibility, managers and administrators must be kept abreast of corporate goals and strategic plans. Managers and administrators must also be thoroughly knowledgeable about each employee's performance history, potential for transfer or advancement, and current career plans.

Managers need to develop a special sensitivity to the career problems of older workers. Dangers of skill obsolescence, job burnout, plateauing and associated loss of motivation, and uncertainty surrounding late career roles and the timing of retirement can diminish the effectiveness of otherwise high-performing senior employees. Middle-aged and older workers are also particularly vulnerable to technological displacement and may suffer greater psychological and financial problems in getting back on a career track.

Many readers may feel that managing their own careers represents a major challenge. They may regard the additional responsibility for guiding the careers of senior employees as an unfair burden. Fortunately, most organizations already have in place personnel policies and practices that can prove quite useful in developing an ongoing career management program. When used regularly, systematic performance appraisal and health appraisal systems provide early warning signals of possible career problems for mid-career and older workers. A well-developed training and development program can help senior employees combat obsolescence and acquire the skills necessary to adjust to changing job requirements. Preretirement planning programs provide employees with help in deciding the timing of retirement. Each of these programs is examined in more detail in the following chapters.

Finally, the implementation of long-term human resource planning coupled with the kinds of career management programs we have described should permit the full utilization of each older worker's special skills, talents, and experience.

Jack Morris pitches for the Detroit Tigers. Jack's pitching performance is objectively reflected in victories and defeats, saves, earned run averages, and strikeouts. Dale Smith runs a drill press in a small machine shop. The shop foreman can easily measure Dale's performance from weekly records of production, quality, wastage, and safety.

Measuring managerial performance, on the other hand, represents a significantly greater challenge. For example, Tom Alston is a 59-year-old mortgage banker with a savings and loan association. Assessment of Tom's performance is more subjective than assessment of the performance of Jack Morris or Dale Smith. For one thing, Tom does not produce a tangible product. The financial decisions that Tom makes often cannot be evaluated for months or even years. Moreover, much of Tom's work is closely integrated with the efforts of other bank officers. Separating Tom's contributions from those of others working on the same projects is nearly impossible. In spite of these difficulties, recommendations still need to be made about the size of Tom's raise, about whether he is promotable, and about how he can best develop his career. These recommendations must be communicated to Tom and must be defensible if Tom challenges them. In a few years, the savings and loan association will also have to consider whether Tom should be encouraged to take early retirement or urged to postpone his retirement. To make effective decisions about Tom's future, management needs an accurate, up-to-date record of his performance and potential.

Effective Assessment Systems

In designing a system for assessment, management must come to grips with a number of key issues, not the least of which is managers' willingness to use the system on a regular basis. Imagine an absolutely elegant performance review system designed by a computer programming genius for a large corporation. Several years and several hundred thousand dollars later, the computerized system is back on the shelf. The complexity of the system overshadowed its elegance, and managers refused to spend the time required to master its intricacies. Experience shows that a straightforward system where managers feel that they have control over the ratings given to employees is much more likely to win acceptance than an overly complex and time-consuming system.

Getting Started and Gaining Acceptance

One way to gain managerial acceptance of a new performance review system and managerial commitment to its use is to ask for managerial input in designing it. The front-end costs of having managers spend a day or two working with personnel specialists to refine and polish a performance review system for use within each department will probably pay dividends in terms of managerial understanding of the system and commitment to its use.

Making performance review a part of every manager's job responsibilities and rewarding managers for conscientiously conducting performance reviews will help ensure that reviews are completed on a timely basis. A top-level management commitment to the use of performance review information in making career decisions demonstrates to others throughout the organization that the review process is considered an important and valued activity.

What to Measure

Managers next need to decide what to measure. Government regulations dictate that performance assessments be based only on job-related behaviors and accomplishments. The first step toward identifying important job-related behaviors is to conduct a job analysis. Job analysis is a systematic process of collecting information through interviews, observations, and questionnaires to isolate the important activities, duties, and responsibilities unique to each position in the organization. Job analysis yields a comprehensive picture of what to measure and forms the basis for designing a performance review system.

Once important job dimensions have been identified, management can set performance standards—the "marginal," "average," or "exceptional" level of performance on each job dimension. Managers then have a common yardstick for rating all employees working on the same job. Comparison of an employee's progress from year to year and comparisons among employees provide an equitable basis for awarding merit increases, making promotion decisions, and diagnosing training needs. Decisions regarding the retention or retirement of older employees can be made consistently and fairly based on performance appraisal records.

Note, however, that job descriptions change over time. Periodic updates of job analysis information and revisions of performance review forms are necessary to reflect changes in job duties and responsibilities. All too often, misunderstandings and disagreements arise when managers and employees do not share a common perception of what is expected and rewarded. Periodic revisions of performance review systems provide an excellent opportunity for managers and employees to clarify expectations and avoid conflicts.

A related issue, and one on which there is little consensus, involves the relative weight that should be assigned to accomplishment (the degree to which objectives have been reached) versus process (how the job is performed on a daily basis). The dilemma here is to recognize and reward individuals who reach or exceed their objectives, yet discourage a "live for today" attitude where employees bend rules, circumvent policies, and sacrifice working relationships with clients and co-workers for the sake of reaching short-run goals. Ideally, a performance review system that captures both the means by which employees carry out their job assignments and the achievement of organizational objectives will permit a balanced evaluation.

Appraisal Formats

Managers and behavioral scientists often disagree about the best appraisal format. A trait format, where managers assess the degree to which employees demonstrate such characteristics as initiative and responsibility, has been quite popular in the past, largely because it is inexpensive and easy to complete. Because trait scales are heavily dependent on managerial inferences and judgments about nonobservable motives, they appear to be particularly vulnerable to subjectivity and bias.

More recently, enthusiasm has mounted for a behavioral observation approach to performance appraisal in which management identifies specific behaviors differentiating effective from ineffective workers. For example, in a sales position, sales managers may perceive that the most successful sales representatives "approach customers immediately," "quickly determine customer needs," and "follow up with customers who postpone purchase decisions." Using the behavioral observation approach, sales managers would rate sales representatives on the degree to which they had been observed demonstrating these desirable behaviors. By focusing sales managers' attention on what employees actually do, not on guesses about their underlying motivations, this approach considers only job-relevant behaviors in judging performance.

Management by objectives (MBO) represents a third approach to performance review. MBO begins with a goal-setting conference between managers and employees, continues with periodic progress checks, and concludes with semiannual reviews of past accomplishments. Advantages of the MBO system include the motivational gains associated with participative goal setting and the establishment of specific, quantifiable criteria for measuring performance.

A fourth approach, often used in conjunction with other formats, requires managers to write a narrative detailing each employee's strengths, weaknesses, and accomplishments during the past review period. Managers are encouraged to keep a diary or log so that selective recall will be minimized in preparing the performance report. While the narrative approach can be both time consuming and subject to bias, it allows each manager to hone in on the behaviors he or she feels are of major importance. Managers recognize the shortcomings of the approach but appreciate the flexibility and control it gives them in evaluating employee performance.

In summary, a number of formats have been suggested for assessing performance. No one format has been found foolproof or bias-free. The choice of an appraisal system depends on the nature of the job, the purpose of employee appraisal, the available opportunities to observe employees' behavior and accomplishments, and numerous other organizational considerations. Although it is impossible to prescribe the one best approach to performance assessment, management must continue experimenting with and evaluating various assessment systems in order to find the system that best meets organizational needs for accurate, objective measures of employee performance.

Assessing Potential

It has long been recognized that the best engineer does not make the best research and development administrator and that the best salesperson does not make the best district sales manager. In fact, the well-known Peter Principle pokes fun at those whose success in lower-level positions leads to promotion followed by mediocrity in higher-level jobs. In order to identify potential for promotion, particularly for managerial positions, a growing number of companies are relying on an assessment center approach. Assessment centers provide an opportunity to observe potential by placing candidates for promotion in a series of situations designed to simulate the problems encountered in higher-level positions. Typically, assessment center simulations include an in-basket exercise, designed to measure administrative, decision-making, delegation, and problem-solving skills; a leaderless discussion group to test communication and teamwork; and stress tests to assess candidates' abilities to think clearly under pressure. Candidates are judged by a group of assessors, higher-level executives and consultants who have been trained to spot promotion potential.

While the assessment center approach can be costly and time-consuming, the opportunity it provides to preview the talents of aspiring candidates under realistic conditions may be worth the price. Assessment center appraisals not only provide management with valuable information about the likely promotability of employees but also provide a good basis for identifying individual training and development needs.

Training Raters

Recognizing the difficulties that most managers experience both with the rating process and with follow-up sessions, many organizations have initiated special training workshops that are designed to help managers make better use of the performance appraisal system. One segment of the typical training program concentrates on helping managers to identify and eliminate biases that might contaminate the objectivity of their judgments. The workshop format illustrates and discusses "halo effect," where managerial evaluations on one dimension of performance unduly influence judgments of all other dimensions of performance; "leniency effect," where managers inflate ratings for most employees; and "central tendency," where managers rate all employees as average or acceptable. Managers learn to guard against these and other sources of bias. The objective of the training workshops is to teach managers the importance of accurately differentiating among weak and effective employees when completing the performance review.

A second and perhaps more challenging dimension of rater training focuses on the performance appraisal feedback sessions between managers and subordinates. In this segment of the training, managers learn to listen, to minimize employee defensiveness, to diagnose work-related difficulties, to solve problems, to set goals for improved performance, and to follow up on employee progress. During these workshop sessions, managers are shown how to aid employees in diagnosing their own strengths and weaknesses and how to develop appropriate and realistic career paths.

Participants in performance appraisal training workshops generally report that although the insights and skills are useful, the conflicts that arise from playing the role of both judge and coach are not easily resolved. As a way around this dilemma, a few experts recommend holding two separate feedback sessions with each subordinate, one to discuss performance and rewards, the other to chart future career moves.

Avoiding Litigation

As we have noted, information based on periodic performance reviews often provides the basis for a variety of managerial actions, including raises, promotions, transfers, retirements, and terminations. When these actions are perceived by employees to be inequitable or biased, the potential exists for grievances and litigation. Recently, researchers have identified characteristics of performance appraisal systems that were associated with outcomes favorable to the company in actual court cases involving performance appraisal. In other words, the researchers learned what facets of a performance review system were statistically associated with successful defenses against charges of bias and discrimination.

On the basis of a study of 66 legal cases in which the use of performance appraisals was at issue in charges of employment discrimination, four characteristics of performance appraisal systems were found to be associated with verdicts in favor of the defendants: (1) evaluators using the system were provided with specific guidelines on how to conduct the performance assessment; (2) the appraisal format was behaviorally oriented rather than trait oriented; (3) the content of the appraisal was developed on the basis of a job analysis; and (4) employees had an opportunity to review the results of their appraisals.[1]

Although not specifically mentioned in this research, another frequently cited characteristic of effective performance review systems is the creation of an appeal mechanism. While the existence of such a mechanism does not ensure that employees will accept their evaluations, providing employees with an opportunity to file a dissenting opinion can clear up mistakes and misunderstandings quickly, before they reach litigation. Moreover, appeal channels that provide for a review of evaluations by higher-level company officials make raters more accountable and perhaps more careful when conducting their evaluations.

Finally, managers should take particular care to justify and document extreme evaluations. A very negative evaluation that adversely affects the career status of an older worker, for example, would probably come under close scrutiny in the event of a grievance or a charge of age bias. Accordingly, a written record with corroborating evaluations from other managers will help offset charges that a particular manager's ratings reflect prejudice or vindictiveness.

Unfortunately, the performance appraisal systems used by many companies fail to incorporate one or more of these characteristics. A recent study showed that more than half of the 217 companies surveyed developed performance appraisal systems without the benefit of a comprehensive job analysis and that more than 60 percent based evaluations on employee traits. Other studies found that more than half of the firms using performance appraisal provided no training for evaluators and that about 10 percent of these firms withheld the results of assessments from employees. Clearly, performance appraisal systems in these companies are particularly vulnerable in the event of discrimination litigation. Moreover, these companies run the risk of making poor and costly business decisions on the basis of questionable performance appraisal data.

---

[1]H.S. Field and W. W. Holley, "The Relationship of Performance Appraisal System Characteristics to Verdicts in Selected Employment Cases," *Academy of Management Journal* 25 (1982), pp. 392–406.

Assessment and Retirement Decisions

As we have noted, Congress has raised the minimum permissible mandatory retirement age from 65 to 70 and has eliminated the retirement age limit entirely for federal employees. Since retirement at age 65 is no longer assured, managers no longer can ignore the problem of older workers whose performance has declined. Managers are now confronted with the need to make retirement decisions on an individualized basis. For each older worker, decisions must be made regarding the form and timing of various steps in the retirement decision process, with attendant risks and stresses for both the employer and the employee. Erroneous decisions permitting poorly performing older workers to postpone retirement can lower productivity, impair the morale of co-workers, and drive up payroll costs. Forcing the retirement of older workers capable of making a productive contribution entails the loss of valued resources as well as economic and psychological costs to the older workers themselves.

For employees who wish to extend their working life beyond age 65, retirement decisions should be based on the performance and health of the employees and on organizational human resource needs. Allowing factors unrelated to the job to influence retirement decisions could set dangerous precedents and create potential inequities for older workers. In extreme cases, biases in retirement decisions could lead to costly litigation. Accordingly, it is imperative for management to identify and eliminate the influence of extraneous factors on retirement decisions.

During the past few years, we have conducted several research studies on how retirement decisions are made. We have learned that even in the age range between 60 and 70, employee age and other characteristics unrelated to performance influence decisions to retain or retire individual older workers. We have also learned that how performance and health data are recorded can influence decisions regarding the timing of retirement. Our findings suggest the need for a careful reexamination of the entire retirement decision process, with particular emphasis on developing job- and health-related decision rules as a basis for making retirement decisions.

Effects of Employee Race, Sex, and
Personal Circumstances

Our first study examined the effects of employee race, sex, and four non-job-related personal characteristics on retirement decisions. The study consisted of a series of retirement decision problems that were presented to personnel administrators in a simulation. Imbedded in the simulation were four cases depicting requests from employees to postpone their retirement beyond age 65. A Personnel Brief was presented for each employee. Each brief contained biographical information, performance data, medical records, and notes from a recent interview.

Race and sex were manipulated by means of pictures. Photographs of older black, white, male, and female employees were included in alternative versions of the Personnel Briefs. The photographs, depicting older persons in appropriate business attire, were matched in order to minimize possible differences in attractiveness. Information pertaining to employee financial status, social adjustment, political activities, and union support was manipulated by varying interviewer comments on the Personnel Briefs.

A national sample of 252 personnel administrators made retirement recommendations for four employees based on information contained in four Personnel Briefs. Employee race, sex, and personal characteristics were systematically varied in each of the briefs. For all of the alternative briefs, the information pertaining to performance records, medical history, and seniority was identical.

The findings indicated that race and sex did not have a systematic effect on retirement decisions. However, the personal and life circumstances of employees significantly influenced the decisions regarding their retirement status. Postponement of retirement was favored more frequently for a 65-year-old employee who was depicted as financially troubled than for a 65-year-old employee with an identical health and performance record who was depicted as financially well off. Continued employment was favored more frequently for an employee who was depicted as likely to make a poor social adjustment to retirement than for an employee who was depicted as likely to adjust well to retirement. Extension of the retirement age was more likely to be permitted for an employee whose personal activities were compatible with business interests than for an employee whose personal activities were in conflict with business interests. Finally, employees whose requests for continuation received union support were treated more favorably than employees whose requests for continuation were opposed by the union.

When taken together, our findings suggest that a variety of factors not directly linked to employee performance affect decisions to retain or retire senior employees who want to stay on. It might be argued that decisions to retain older employees who would otherwise suffer financial or emotional hardship represent particularly humanistic flexibility. Similarly, the retention of older employees who publicly espouse probusiness attitudes might be viewed as an appropriate reward for loyalty and commitment. Consideration of the union position on continuation of employees beyond age 65 may reflect a realistic strategy for maintaining harmonious industrial relations. However, a precedent is established by each of the retention decisions made on these bases. Consideration of such non-work-related characteristics as financial position and social adjustment creates potential inequities and leaves the organization vulnerable to charges of bias, favoritism, and discrimination. Accordingly, management may need to have carefully developed and communicated criteria for the retention of older employees, along with well-developed systems for careful and consistent implementation of these criteria.

Effects of Appraisal Format, Age, and Performance Level

Our second study examined the effects of performance appraisal format, age, and performance level on retirement decisions.[2] A major objective was to determine whether the particular form in which performance appraisal information is coded and presented affects how the information is assimilated and weighted in retirement decisions. With respect to retention or retirement decisions, some performance appraisal formats may be more resistant than others to the potentially biasing effects of employee characteristics such as age. In this study, the strategy was to examine the effects of three commonly used performance appraisal formats—management by objectives (MBO), behaviorally anchored rating scales (BARS), and trait scales—on the judgments of personnel decision makers for employees who differed in age and whose performance was summarized in one of these formats.

The participants were required to make retirement evaluations and decisions for three employees on the basis of simulated job information, personnel records, and performance appraisal data. The age of the employees was set at 58, 65, or 69. Their performance level was high, medium, or low. A traits, BARS, or MBO appraisal format was used.

We found that the performance appraisal format did not influence retirement recommendations. This finding suggests that managers will make similar interpretations of performance appraisal results regardless of whether these results are presented in the BARS, traits, or MBO format. Employee age, however, affected the retirement recommendations. There was a greater willingness to postpone retirement for younger employees (age 58) than for identically qualified older employees (ages 65 and 69). Older employees with marginal performance records were particularly likely to be recommended for retirement. It appears that the retirement decision process is unlikely to pose difficulties when employees are performing their jobs well, but when employee performance is low or

---
[2]B. Rosen, T. H. Jerdee, and R. O. Lunn, "Effects of Performance Appraisal Format, Age, and Performance Level on Retirement Decisions," *Journal of Applied Psychology* 66 (1981), pp. 515-19.

questionable, the problem of deciding among the available retirement options becomes much more difficult.

A practical implication of these findings is that a good way to minimize problems in the retirement decision process is to manage other components of the personnel system effectively so that there are few instances of mediocre or low performance among older workers. The importance of a good career management system cannot be overemphasized. One expert, for example, has called for a new form of human resource development that takes age factors into account. Under this proposal, declining performance would be counteracted by a series of skills upgrading and retraining programs geared to the special needs of older employees.

Another practical implication of these findings is that more work needs to be done on the provision of constructive options for older employees whose performance is not high. For these employees, decision makers usually eschew termination in favor of the status quo. In many instances, neither termination nor continuation in the present position is desirable. More suitable options, including job changes and work phaseout approaches, need to be considered. Further work is needed on the development and testing of flexible alternatives to termination or the status quo. We shall consider these flexible retirement alternatives in greater detail in Chapter 8.

Our findings in this study also provide further evidence that employee age has important effects on judgments and decisions in regard to employee retirement. These age effects are definitely to the disadvantage of the employee who is nearing the mandatory retirement age of 70.

Effects of Health and Age

Our third study was concerned with the effects of health information on retirement decisions.[3] Information on employee health is typically assessed by physicians and nurses and recorded in personnel files. The information is then used by managers to aid them in determining future employability. Both the nature of the information and the way in which it is presented may have effects on retirement decisions. This study was concerned specifically with the effects on retirement decisions of (1) the perspective taken in portraying health information (emphasizing capacities or emphasizing disabilities); (2) the job relevance of the health condition; and (3) employee age.

Employee health data are subject to potential distortions and misinterpretations that mask the degree to which workers are capable of meeting

---

[3]R. O. Lunn, "The Effects of Age, Manner of Presentation of Health Data, and Job Relevance of the Health Condition on Retirement and Retention Decisions," unpublished doctoral dissertation, University of North Carolina, 1981.

job demands. For example, managers may overestimate the disabling effects of various medical conditions. Medical reports that emphasize the capacities (what an employee can do) as opposed to the disabilities (what an employee cannot do) associated with particular health conditions are likely to influence retirement decisions in a direction more favorable, and hence more fair, to older workers.

Fair and equitable retirement decisions require careful consideration of the relevance of health conditions to job requirements. It is important to determine the degree to which health problems represent serious handicaps for meeting specific job requirements. In some situations, the existence of various health disorders or physical impairments may prevent continuation in a particular job. For example, a severe hernia might prevent the continuation of a laborer. The same impairment would be much less likely to prevent the continuation of a clerical employee. Clearly, an employee's ability to continue working depends to a large extent on the degree to which a medical disorder is a serious impairment to functioning in a specific position.

Managerial misinterpretation of health information on older employees may be particularly likely because of commonly held stereotypes regarding the declining health of older people. Accordingly, identical health conditions may be perceived as more serious and disabling for older workers than for younger workers.

The research approach was to present a series of case problems to 321 personnel administrators in the context of a retirement decision exercise. The participants were provided with personnel files consisting of work histories, performance assessment information, and health data for four employees, each working in a different job and having one of the following health problems: rheumatoid arthritis, depression reaction, cardiac problem, and ulcer. The participants were required to determine the employment or retirement status of each employee. Alternative versions of the cases contained manipulations of the three independent variables: (1) emphasis on capacities versus disabilities in health reports; (2) relevance of the health condition for meeting job demands; and (3) employee age.

The health reports were in the form of letters from physicians. In one version, emphasizing capacities, the physician's letter was written in terms of what the employee could do (for example: "May lift up to 50 lbs."). In another version, emphasizing disabilities, the physician's letter was written in terms of what the employee could not do (for example: "May not lift more than 50 lbs."). Note that in both versions the health condition is equally severe. Each participant received health reports emphasizing worker capacity in two cases and emphasizing worker limitations in the other two cases.

Manipulation of the job relevance of health conditions was accomplished by presenting job descriptions written in two versions. In the high-relevance version, the health condition was obviously relevant to the particular job requirement. For example, a heart condition would obviously be relevant to a position that requires the lifting of heavy mail sacks. In the low-relevance condition, the same health condition was not relevant to the particular job requirements. For example, the heart condition might not be relevant to a position involving automated mail sorting and distribution. In other words, alternative versions of job descriptions were created that differed only in the degree to which the job requirements were potential barriers for the individual with the health problem. The participants reviewed two cases where health problems were job relevant and two cases where health problems were not job relevant.

The age of the employee, manipulated through alternative versions of the employment records, was depicted as 55, 62, or 69. Each participant reviewed cases depicting employees at three different ages.

The respondents were asked to choose one of the following alternatives as the recommended action:

1. Continue in present position (at full salary and benefits).
2. Transfer to a less demanding position (at 75 percent of current salary and benefits).
3. Assign to part-time position (at 50 percent of salary and benefits).
4. Phase out (reduce immediately to part-time at 50 percent of salary and benefits; progressively reduce the time worked to complete termination with accrued pension benefits within 12 months).
5. Terminate (with accrued pension benefits).

We found that health reports emphasizing capacities were associated with high recommendations for continuation and that health reports emphasizing disabilities were associated with recommendations for part-time assignment, phaseout, and termination. These findings suggest that retirement decisions are more favorable to the older employee when health reports emphasize functional capacities than when they emphasize functional disabilities.

The specific job requirements had complex effects on the recommendation of various retirement options. As expected, continuation was favored when health was not relevant to the job requirements, and transfer was favored when health was a potential handicap for meeting the job requirements.

As in our previous research, we found consistent age effects on retirement decisions. The recommendations reflected a strong desire to continue or transfer the 55-year-old and 62-year-old employees and to reassign to part-time status, phase out, or terminate the 69-year-old employee.

With the minimum permissible mandatory retirement age advanced to 70, the determination of an older worker's employment status may depend to a great extent on his or her ability to contribute to organizational goals and objectives. Predictions about future contributions are likely to be extrapolated from information regarding past performance and health. Earlier in this chapter, we discussed strategies for improving the objectivity and defensibility of performance review systems. The findings from our study of the interpretation of medical information suggest that much can also be done to improve current practices with respect to the assessment of health potential.

Those findings indicate that a major source of decision bias is misinterpretation of medical data. Specifically, when medical reports emphasized capacities (functions that an employee could successfully perform), the recommendations favored continued employment. When medical reports emphasized disabilities (limitations and restrictions on the functions that an employee could successfully perform), the recommendations favored part-time assignments, phaseouts, and termination. Moreover, in some instances employees were recommended for phaseout or termination even when their health problems were not likely to interfere with their ability to meet job demands.

The problem of assessing the implications of various medical disorders for the performance of specific job functions obviously needs much more attention. While certain extremely serious medical disabilities may preclude continued employment in any capacity, other medical disabilities may constrain performance to a much more limited extent. Our findings suggest that in some instances management may not adequately differentiate the degrees to which medical problems are handicaps for specific job functions. Of particular concern are the failures of management to recognize that reductions in certain physical capacities may make little or no difference for successful job performance. Failures to differentiate the job relevance of various health problems worked to the particular disadvantage of older workers.

New Health Guidelines

Managers concerned with helping senior employees should consider a systematic and comprehensive approach to evaluation of health, including the following:

1. Developing current and complete job descriptions, with particular emphasis on identifying the physical and psychological demands associated with each job.
2. Evaluating current procedures for recording and maintaining medical histories. Encouraging medical practitioners to develop a balanced approach that emphasizes both employee capacities and employee

limitations associated with illness or injury. Redesigning medical reporting forms to focus on the job-related implications of medical problems.

3. Creating workshops and seminars for both medical professionals and managers to improve interpretations of medical histories and to increase the accuracy of decisions regarding further employability.
4. Establishing training sessions to help managers identify and eliminate the potential influences of age stereotypes, bias, and discrimination from evaluations of performance and health.
5. Experimenting with job redesign as a strategy for maintaining the employability and productivity of senior workers with health problems.

The implementation of these procedures should help managers make more accurate and objective assessments of each individual's health status and future employability.

Summary

In order to cope with rapid organizational changes brought about by the technological revolution, foreign competition, and uncertain economic conditions, corporate planners will be forced to rethink their human resource management strategies. During a transition period, severe shortages in some jobs are likely, while workers whose skills are in less demand will compete for the remaining jobs in their industries. At the managerial level, difficult choices must be made regarding the retention, retraining, or replacement of hundreds of thousands of employees.

These managerial decisions should be made on the basis of organizational staffing projections and individual abilities and potentials to contribute. Valid information regarding individual performance, potential, and health should be collected and analyzed as a basis for making these important decisions. Particularly problematic are decisions regarding the continuation or retirement of older employees. Management no longer can avoid the evaluation of senior employees in anticipation of retirement at age 65. On the other hand, management may need to offer special incentives to encourage older workers with highly valued skills and experience to postpone their retirement plans.

Many companies need to reexamine their current practices for assessing performance and health and for using performance and health assessments in the decision process. A few companies have already started to address these issues, appointing task forces and study committees to evaluate the legality and effectiveness of current policies and to recommend policy revisions where necessary. Their lead should be followed.

Combating Obsolescence

Main Issues

- Obsolescence should be combated by treating human resources as renewable assets.
- Training and development to prevent obsolescence must be tied in with organizational strategic plans.

- Training and development needs must be systematically assessed at all career stages.
- Specialized training programs should be available for almost all employee groups at all career stages.

We are confident that in future years high-performing older workers will not encounter resistance to extending their retirement dates. Indeed, we expect organizations to revise retirement policies and create new incentives to encourage these experienced and dedicated older employees to remain on the job. However, for employees whose performance declines in late career stages, corporate doors may be closed and locked.

The performance of some older workers declines in the twilight of their careers because they lose motivation. The performance of many others, however, declines because their skills and knowledge have become outdated. This problem is likely to get worse before long. According to futurists, in coming years many different kinds of professionals will be forced to drop out of the work force every four or five years for extensive retooling and retraining. Who is responsible for career obsolescence? More importantly, what can corporate planners, line managers, and individual senior employees do to combat obsolescence? In this chapter, we examine the growing problems of obsolescence and the creative approaches that some companies are using to keep their employees' skills and knowledge up to date.

What is Obsolescence?

Behavioral scientists have identified two types of obsolescence, job obsolescence and worker obsolescence. Jobs become obsolete and gradually disappear when demands for certain products or services decline or new manufacturing techniques replace older, less efficient processes. For example, the jobs of buggy whip makers and blacksmiths have pretty much disappeared over the last half century. In future years, quality control inspectors may be replaced by optical scanners and door-to-door salespeople will probably give way to computerized shop-at-home services. In the meantime, Labor Department projections of demands for various skills help vocational counselors steer job seekers away from jobs on the occupational endangered species list.

Individual obsolescence refers to a gradual reduction in work effectiveness. When employees fall behind in understanding how to use new tools and techniques or fail to recognize how the application of new knowledge can improve their performance, they become vulnerable to obsolescence. The term *half-life*, borrowed from nuclear physics, has been used as a rough measure of obsolescence across occupations. A half-life is the time it takes for individuals to lose about half of their competence due to changes in knowledge and technology. The half-life of information workers, engineers, and scientists may be as short as five years. Lawyers, physicians, and accountants are also vulnerable to rapid change in their fields. Managers and administrators who have fallen behind in their understanding of computer technology, the changing regulatory environment, and the internationalization of businesses will experience individual obsolescence. Note that the rate of obsolescence among employees varies across occupations and within job categories. Accordingly, individual obsolescence may go unnoticed for years.

Obviously, senior employees are particularly vulnerable to both job obsolescence and individual obsolescence. The greater vulnerability of older workers to job obsolescence is reflected in the longer period of unemployment that older workers typically experience after job phaseouts and plant shutdowns. Moreover, older employees with substantial family and financial obligations cannot easily move into lengthy retraining programs. With respect to individual obsolescence, managers may come to take for granted a senior employee's abilities to contribute. Compounding the problem, the senior employee may be reluctant to admit that certain skills have become rusty or may fear that learning new methods, procedures, or techniques is too much of a challenge. The problem is exacerbated by corporate reluctance to invest in upgrading the skills of senior employees.

In a rapidly changing business environment, obsolescence represents a costly problem. Neglecting the problem may make it even more costly. Imagine the costs associated with executive obsolescence and incompetence. Poor decisions, alienated clients, and demoralized subordinates carry a hefty price. For the executives themselves, the psychological costs of feeling outdated include loss of self-esteem, insecurity, and stress.

When such costs are multiplied by the number of executive, professional, technical, and operative employees whose skills and job knowledge have gradually declined, the costs to organizations and to society are staggering.

The Roots of Obsolescence

A very small number of organizations have developed reputations for bringing in "the best and the brightest," milking them for every drop of creativity, putting them out to pasture at an early age, and repeating the cycle. In the vast majority of organizations, however, obsolescence most likely results from sins of omission rather than sins of commission. Two of the most serious organizational sins of omission are failing to recognize the symptoms of obsolescence and failing to make the necessary investments in training and development.

Managers concerned with how their own organizational or departmental policies foster or offset obsolescence need look no further than their human resource management philosophy. Are individuals perceived as depreciating goods with only a limited useful life, or are they perceived as assets that will continue to grow if managed properly?

The depreciation model of human resource management implies that an individual's value to the organization peaks at early career stages, plateaus at mid-career, and steadily declines thereafter. According to the philosophy underlying the depreciation model, investments in training and development beyond the mid-career stage are not likely to be cost effective.

The depreciation model of human resource management may lead to myopic decisions. The depreciation model fails to consider turnover costs, which include the costs of recruiting, selecting, socializing, developing, and compensating a new employee. In one division of the General Electric Company, for example, replacement costs were found to be very high. GE discovered that retraining an engineer could be accomplished for less than one third the cost of hiring a new one. According to one industrial psychologist, the odds are 5 to 1 that a newly hired college graduate will leave the organization within five years. The odds are substantially better that a 50-year-old will stay with the organization for the next 15 years. The value of the increased commitment, loyalty, and experience of senior employees whose careers have remained on track because of early problem diagnosis and effective career management should not be underestimated.[1]

An alternative to the depreciation model is to consider human re-

---

[1] Wayne Cascio, *Costing Human Resources* (Boston: Kent Publishing, 1982).

sources as renewable assets that will continue to yield a high rate of return for a long time if managed properly. This model requires that managers take the necessary steps to preserve and renew the value of human assets. In a recent article, Senator Edward Kennedy captured the philosophy underlying the asset model when he said, "We must also adopt a new strategy of investment in human capital—in the education of our children and the skills of our workers. . . . Our capital stock consists not only of iron and steel, but of brains and knowledge."[2]

We conceive of the preservation and renewal of human assets as a three-dimensional problem. The first dimension requires comprehensive career planning, as described in Chapter 5. The second dimension focuses on early diagnosis of the symptoms of obsolescence by means of objective performance and health assessment, as discussed in Chapter 6. The third dimension requires effective intervention when assessment results indicate the need for training and development to counteract the onset of obsolescence.

Organizations committed to preserving the value of their human assets might consider a variety of innovative approaches to training and development.

Corporate Efforts to Combat Obsolescence

Preventive maintenance has become widely established in many settings. Engineers have developed timetables for periodic checkups and parts replacement for production equipment. Governmental departments of transportation monitor highway erosion and schedule road resurfacing. We call the tuner when our piano begins to sound off-key, and we go to the dentist and to the family physician for periodic checkups. In each of these instances, we try to prevent a problem from developing or getting worse. Both in the corporate world and in our personal lives, we adhere to the old saw "An ounce of prevention is worth a pound of cure."

Corporate preventive maintenance with respect to the skills and knowledge of human resources at every organizational level can similarly prevent costly problems of obsolescence, motivational loss, and career stagnation. Accordingly, more and more organizations are starting to develop comprehensive programs of skills upgrading and retraining to help each employee work at full potential. We now examine a model program for maintaining the employability of senior employees. It is based on a composite of corporate efforts in many organizations.

---

[2]Edward M. Kennedy, "The Challenges before Us," *American Psychologist* 39, no. 1 (January 1984), p. 65.

A Model Program: Training and Development at Multitech

Multitech is a high-technology multinational corporation that manufactures computers, copiers, and communication equipment. The corporate structure at Multitech can best be characterized as a matrix design. Scientists, engineers, financial analysts, marketing specialists, and production personnel are drawn from various departments to work on projects and task forces. A project might involve the development of a desk-size portable copier or the design of a complex radar system. Project teams work together for periods ranging from several months to five years. Project work is intensive, limiting the time available for professional development.

Recognizing the importance of a comprehensive effort to combat career obsolescence, human resource planners at Multitech have developed a corporate-wide, comprehensive program for skills upgrading and professional development. Key elements of the program are illustrated in Figure 7-1.

As shown in Figure 7-1, Multitech's plan for combating career obsolescence begins with a thorough assessment of training and development needs. Inputs into the needs assessment include corporate human resource plans; performance appraisal results; survey data gathered from executives, managers, and employees; and recommendations from training and development advisory panels.

Review of Corporate Human Resource Plans

In Chapter 5, we described how organizations go about developing human resource plans. Corporate strategic plans provide a basis for projecting the mix of skills, talent, and experience needed to reach short- and long-range corporate goals. Comparison of the distribution of skills in the present work force with projected future requirements provides a starting point for identifying future training requirements. Moreover, by examining career aspirations and plans, human resource managers can identify those individuals who appear to have the interest and motivation for training and development. Identification of future needs from human resource projections represents a proactive approach to training or retraining.

Review of Performance Assessment Results

Returning to Figure 7-1, performance assessment results provide a second source of information regarding training and development needs. As

---

FIGURE 7-1

Training and Development of Human Resources: Multitech's Plan for Combating Career Obsolescence

I. Assessment of training and development needs
   Review of corporate human resource plans
   Review of performance assessment results
   Opinion survey on training and development needs
   Review by advisory council

II. Designing of training and development programs
   Scientific and technical training
   Management development
   Training for production and administrative employees
   Corporate-wide programs
   Retirement-related programs

III. Evaluation and review

IV. Long-range planning

---

noted in Chapter 6, data derived from performance appraisals and assessment centers signal an early warning for detecting special needs for skills upgrading or retraining. Alert managers can use performance review data to diagnose specific training requirements for individual employees, for groups of employees, or for entire departments. Early intervention with employees whose performance assessments indicate declines in productivity or quality often prevents more serious performance problems in the future.

Opinion Survey on Training and Development Needs

Another approach to assessing training and development needs at Multitech involves annual surveys of executives, managers, and employees. At every organizational level, results from a training needs survey pinpoint special interests and problem areas. For example, last year executives mentioned an interest in several types of training, including more intensive preparation for foreign assignments, additional training in representing the company to the media, and new stress management programs. Managers requested refresher courses in communication, problem solving, and conflict resolution. Production employees indicated a desire to participate in training programs designed to enhance their contributions to quality circles. Each of these items was identified through responses to the training needs survey.

Review by Advisory Council

Multitech has also formed a Training and Development Advisory Council. On this panel sit representatives from the human resource department, key department heads, project managers, a union official, and a university professor who directs his school's Executive Development Program. The panel meets quarterly to identify business trends, map out the implications of these trends for future training and development activity, and recommend topics for future corporate workshops, seminars, or training programs. Over the past 15 years, the advisory council has recommended affirmative action workshops, preretirement planning programs, career management seminars, international business workshops, and government regulation seminars.

Since resources for training and development are limited, each year corporate planners and personnel officials collect various suggestions for training and development programs, develop budget estimates for each program, assign priorities, and make plans to implement the programs that are expected to contribute most to short- and long-run organizational goals. In developing a training and development curriculum for the coming year, planners at Multitech attempt to consider the special needs of employees in various job classifications. As shown in Figure 7–1, ongoing programs are developed and maintained for scientific and technical personnel, management, and production and administrative employees. In addition, training and development programs also reflect the needs of women, minority, and senior employees. Many of Multitech's programs are open to all employees in the organization.

Each program has the overriding objective of preparing employees to fill their present positions more effectively or to assume more challenging assignments in the future. Here is a look at some of the specific programs offered by Multitech.

Scientific and Technical Training at Multitech

Corporate planners at Multitech recognized many years ago that scientists and engineers in its various divisions found it particularly difficult to keep abreast of innovations and breakthroughs in their disciplines. Scientific and technical employees were therefore targeted for participation in a comprehensive and continuing upgrading and retraining program.

These employees were encouraged to participate actively in professional associations. Multitech reimbursed association dues, developed a plan to underwrite subscriptions to scholarly journals, and provided paid time off and travel support so that scientists and engineers could attend conferences and workshops. In addition, Multitech targeted a special series, "Science in Progress," to senior research and development personnel.

The series consisted of 15 half-day presentations on current developments and cutting-edge scientific issues. The presentations were made by university researchers, visiting international scholars, and engineers and scientists in other Multitech divisions.

At first, several of the senior scientists who had been with the company for 20 or more years felt uncomfortable about returning to the classroom. One admitted that his discomfort was based in part on concerns about looking outdated to younger colleagues. When training managers learned about these attitudes, they alerted workshop leaders to create a supportive learning climate for senior participants by drawing on their experience and know-how.

The reactions of the participating scientific and technical employees were unanimously positive. Several recommended that "Science in Progress" be conducted on a three-year cycle and that new topics and issues be introduced each time it was presented. A follow-up of the participants by the training staff revealed that their interest in keeping current had been heightened by the series. The participants reported taking increased advantage of the outside learning opportunities provided by evening courses, professional association seminars, and journals. The enthusiasm of the first group of graduates spread throughout the company. The success of the series was reflected in overenrollments each time it was repeated.

Management Development

A second group targeted for comprehensive and continuous development activities was the cadre of managerial personnel at Multitech. The matrix or project organizational structure necessitated a high degree of flexibility among managers. In order to deal with a diverse group of employees with various technical backgrounds, managers had to remain abreast of management principles in the areas of planning, goal setting, scheduling, motivation, communication, and conflict resolution. The project managers at Multitech work under tight deadlines and endure considerable stress. Consequently, human resource planners consider it especially important to offer them extensive opportunities to sharpen and enhance their skills.

Management training and development take a variety of forms at Multitech. The training staff has designed a continuous series of in-house workshops. Full-day and half-day seminars are offered in corporate classrooms throughout the year. Managers are required to participate in a minimum of 40 hours of continuing education programs each year. They sign up for the workshops that interest them. The titles of the workshops offered during the past year give a good indication of the available breadth of topics. Recent titles include "The Art of Negotiation," "Coping with Managerial Stress," "Better Speechmaking," "Creative Problem Solving," and "Financial Planning with the Personal Computer."

Moving beyond short courses, Multitech has also created a longer management development course for senior managers. Managers attend a three-week training experience that focuses on potential problems unique to Multitech's organizational design and technology. Cases and problems likely to be encountered in the various Multitech divisions are analyzed and discussed. Realism is enhanced further through interactive computer simulations that enable managers to examine potential consequences of their decisions. Multitech trainers feel that the future orientation of the course provides an excellent opportunity to help managers identify and prepare for the managerial challenges awaiting them in future years.

Multitech encourages and supports managers who wish to attend university-based executive programs. Managers are given released time to participate in these programs. The participants often indicate that the opportunity to interact and share ideas with managers from other organizations proves as valuable as the formal classroom instruction.

As part of its management development efforts, each year Multitech provides support to enable a few managers to attend university summer courses in the liberal arts. Managers welcome the chance that this gives them to gain a broader perspective on business issues by studying philosophy, literature, and the arts. The managers who attend such courses report that this return to the classroom is a rejuvenating experience.

Finally, Multitech makes an intense effort to individualize training, fitting the kind of training and development experiences to the special needs of each manager. It uses a management-by-objectives system for evaluating managerial performance. Every quarter, managers meet with their superiors to set goals and objectives for the coming three-month period. Along with their performance goals, managers are required to establish goals for personal development. Several payoffs of building personal development goals into the MBO system have been identified by Multitech managers, one of which is that putting these goals in writing forces managers to give serious consideration to their own training needs. At Multitech, the achievement of personal development goals is rewarded in the same way as the achievement of sales or manufacturing goals.

Training for Production and Administrative Employees

Each year, Multitech phases out certain manual operations in favor of automated assembly processes. Employees who will be displaced in these phaseouts are given technical training for up to 30 weeks, sometimes on-site and sometimes at the company's national training facility in North

Carolina. And in still other instances, employees receive tuition assistance and a training stipend to attend specialized evening programs at technical institutes in their region.

Multitech's own administrative staff is typically the first to test the company's new high-technology office equipment. Hands-on experience with the latest office technology requires that administrative personnel undergo almost continuous retraining. While some administrative employees have noted that they barely have time to master a piece of equipment before it is replaced by a more complex model, almost all of them agree that the experience provides invaluable training and quickly eliminates the fear of technological change.

Corporate-Wide Programs

Multitech planners are committed to the philosophy that a productive work force requires effective career management and lifelong training. In addition to the formal programs aimed at employees in various occupational categories, Multitech uses a wide variety of corporate-wide training and development approaches, including divisional training centers, job rotation and internship programs, and informal, on-the-job techniques.

Each of the major Multitech divisions has its own training center. At each center is a library of books, cassettes, movies, and computerized self-instruction materials to help employees keep abreast of new developments. Employees may use the library during lunch periods or after hours, or they may borrow materials from the library for use at home.

Human resource managers at Multitech put a great deal of emphasis on internships and job rotation as training techniques. Age barriers are broken in job rotation and internship assignments. You would be just as likely to find a senior employee collaborating with or working under the supervision of a young scientist, engineer, or manager as to find a senior employee mentoring a junior colleague. Internships and temporary job assignments permit workers of all ages to add to their skills and knowledge and to gain exposure to new corporate problems.

In addition to the formal training approaches used throughout Multitech, each foreman, supervisor, manager, and executive is expected to serve as an informal coach from the very first day of a new employee's tenure. The personnel department has circulated research reports showing that early job challenges are associated with employee desires to continue learning and developing. Through the delegation of challenging assignments and the inclusion of key employees in participative decision making, supervisors at every level of the corporate hierarchy work to sharpen the skills and job knowledge of their subordinates.

Retirement-Related Programs

Another dimension of Multitech's efforts to combat obsolescence is directed specifically at employees nearing retirement age. Going far beyond the traditional workshops designed to help prepare employees for retirement life, the Multitech program focuses on alternatives to complete retirement and on postretirement employment options and second-career opportunities.

Multitech has established its own temporary help pool. Retirees who wish to work on a part-time basis indicate their availability and assignment preferences with the pool coordinator (also a Multitech retiree). Where necessary, Multitech offers refresher courses to employees who have been away from the job for some time. Retired secretaries receive training in word processing, and retired accountants take a refresher course in tax law. Retirees may be called on to fill in during vacation periods or to add their expertise to special projects.

In recent years, Multitech has developed a new tuition reimbursement plan that is designed to help retiring workers prepare for second careers. The plan calls for reimbursing up to $4,000 in educational costs for each employee. Senior employees can begin to draw from this educational fund up to three years before their retirement and can continue to draw from it for three years after retirement. Many employees prepare for second careers that permit a more flexible work schedule. Employees who acquire skills in what Multitech has designated "critical need areas" are often offered postretirement part-time or consulting positions with Multitech.

Evaluation and Review

Programs to combat obsolescence are very expensive. Nationally, organizations in the United States spend more than $130 billion each year for training. This remarkably large outlay reflects the high cost of keeping abreast of change and the managerial commitment to maintaining a fully trained and productive work force. Human resource managers at Multitech must constantly examine the costs and benefits of training expenses.

In the past, Multitech, like many of its competitors, did not conduct very systematic evaluations of its training efforts. Often evaluations were limited to examining participants' reactions to the various programs, workshops, and on-the-job experiences. When trainees responded favorably, a program was considered successful.

Now, however, the Multitech training staff uses much more sophisticated approaches to assess training effectiveness. In some instances, it has employed carefully controlled experiments to compare the career progress and job performance of trainees and a control group of nontrainees. In other instances, the training and accounting staff have collaborated to assess the cost of sending each trainee through a program and the dollar benefits associated with higher-quality work, better decisions, and improved client service.

Multitech has made a commitment to further research on training effectiveness. Recently, behavioral scientists were invited to conduct research to determine what learning pedagogies are most effective with workers in different age categories. The overriding goal is to learn how to maximize the results from each approach to maintaining a productive work force.

Long-Range Planning

Recognizing that in our rapidly changing technological society training must be a never-ending endeavor, planners at Multitech have formulated long-range plans for training and development. They have designed a plan for establishing professional retraining centers around the country. The plan calls for industry and government cosponsorship of regional training centers. High-technology employees will be given a year or more off with salary approximately every 10 years. Scientists, engineers, and executives will use this sabbatical period to attend a regional training center and become recertified in their field of specialization. As Multitech sees the future, dramatic increases in the rate of knowledge creation will make it necessary for knowledge workers to retool every decade.

Summary

As we have noted, Multitech represents a composite of the creative approaches that organizations have implemented to combat employee obsolescence. Not every approach will prove practical or appropriate in every organization. All of the approaches are expensive. Managers are encouraged to consider the trade-offs. Our prediction is that investments in the growth, development, and maintenance of human resources will pay dividends in productivity, quality, and commitment for years to come.

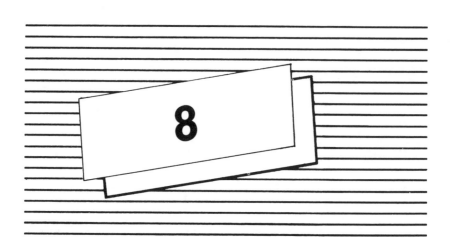

Flexible Retirement Systems

Main Issues

- Many individual, organizational, and governmental factors enter into retirement planning.

- Knowledge of the retirement decision process is needed in order to evaluate proposed policies and to individualize the retirement decision process. Much is known; more knowledge is needed.

- Organizations should aim to provide great flexibility in arrangements for phasing into retirement.

Tom Black is the manager of a Citizens Bank and Trust branch office that is located in a suburb of a large southeastern city. Personnel functions are highly centralized within Citizens Bank and Trust, which means that Tom needs the approval of corporate personnel to deal with most of the staffing problems in his branch office.

During the past few months, Tom has been struggling with two almost opposite staffing concerns: the need to retain an experienced cashier who has announced her upcoming retirement and the need to terminate or to encourage the early retirement of a poorly performing senior loan officer. As Tom pondered these two retirement problems, he realized how little attention he had given to retirement-related issues. He recalled that for many years Citizens Bank and Trust had encouraged older employees to participate in the annual retirement planning workshop. He also recalled that in 1978 the bank had extended the mandatory retirement age to 70 in compliance with new government regulations. Beyond these two incidents, however, he was hard-pressed to think of any changes in corporate retirement policies that had been made during the past decade.

Tom wondered what it would take to induce his best cashier to postpone her retirement plans. Would she consider working on a part-time basis, for example? Would the personnel vice president at headquarters approve of a part-time arrangement? And how would the personnel VP react to offering the poorly performing loan officer a large incentive to take early retirement? Tom had read a good deal lately about the "aging" work force, and he hoped that human resource planners would start giving serious attention to developing new retirement planning approaches. As Tom sized up the situation, more flexible retirement policies were badly needed. Tom wanted policies that would enable him to encourage high-performing employees to postpone retirement and to encourage low performers to take early retirement.

In this chapter, we examine the entire retirement decision process. We develop a model showing how individuals in various occupational, health, and financial categories weigh government and organizational policies in planning their retirement dates. Among the government policies considered are current laws regulating retirement, social security policies, and inflation targets. We also examine how corporate policies, including more flexible retirement options, provide new opportunities for senior employees to extend their careers. Finally, we examine incentives for early retirement. We conclude that there is much room for organizational innovation and experimentation, followed by careful evaluation, to help managers like Tom Black manage the retirement decision process.

In order to help employees make wise retirement decisions, managers must have a good understanding of the individual retirement decision process. In the past, it has been administratively convenient to accept an age-based criterion for retirement decisions, thus forcing the retirement of many senior employees who wished to continue working and were physically and mentally capable of doing so. Recognizing the moral and economic shortcomings of mandatory retirement policies, Congress has prohibited mandatory retirement before age 70 and eliminated the retirement age limit entirely for federal employees. Administration and congressional proposals are now pointing toward complete elimination of mandatory age-based retirement.

To achieve the full potential of this policy of creating new opportunities for older employees, managers will have to develop a much more sophisticated understanding of the individual retirement decision process than was required under the traditional policy of mandatory retirement at age 65. Accordingly, we have developed a model of the individual retirement decision process to summarize important variables that affect the timing of retirement.

Individual Retirement Decision Process

A model of the factors that influence individual retirement intentions is shown in Figure 8–1. The model conceptualizes the formulation of retirement intentions on the basis of a senior employee's evaluation of three major categories of variables: (1) individual, family, and community circumstances; (2) government policies; and (3) organizational policies.

FIGURE 8-1

Model of the Individual Retirement Decision Process

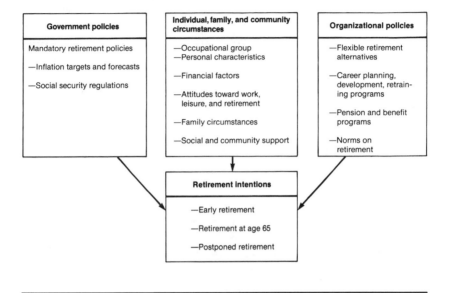

Individual, family, and community circumstances include occupational group; sex, race, educational level, and health; finances; attitudes toward work, leisure, and retirement; family circumstances; and local social and community support systems. At issue here is how various subgroups of individual senior employees respond to government and organizational efforts to maintain their productive employment.

Government policies include laws regulating or preventing age-based mandatory retirement as well as proposed changes in provisions for social security eligibility. Of special concern to managers and corporate planners are the long-run effects that extension of the mandatory retirement age and changes in the earnings provisions for social security eligibility have on the timing of retirement.

Organizational policies include flexible alternatives to retirement such as job changes and part-time work; career planning, development, and retraining for senior workers; pension and benefit program features; and organizational norms concerning the retention of older workers.

In summary, we will systematically consider the effects that the variables denoted in the individual retirement decision model have on retirement intentions. This review should provide important insights on how individual senior employees vary in their reactions to government and organizational policies as they formulate their retirement intentions.

Effects of Employee Variables

Our model of the individual retirement decision process, depicted in Exhibit 8-1, shows that governmental and organizational policies will probably have different effects on the planning of retirement, depending on the individual's life circumstances. For example, changes in social security regulations designed to provide financial incentives for continuing work beyond age 65 would have different effects on the retirement intentions of individuals in different financial circumstances. Similarly, flexible retirement options might have less appeal for a worker with serious health problems than for a similarly situated worker in excellent health.

The decision model shows categories of demographic variables associated with intentions to elect early retirement, on-time retirement, or postponed retirement. The following categories of variables will be considered:

a. Occupations.
b. Personal characteristics—sex, race, educational level, and health.
c. Financial situation—source and magnitude of postretirement income.
d. Attitudes toward work, leisure, and retirement.
e. Family circumstances (marital status, employment status of spouse, number and ages of dependents).
f. Local social and community support for continued employment, in the form of convenient public transportation, special services for the elderly, health care provisions, and leisure-time activities.

We will review what is currently known about the relationship of these variables to retirement behavior. Our goal is to help managers predict the likely timing of retirement among various subgroups of older employees.

Occupation

Occupational status has been found to be associated with retirement intentions. Blue-collar workers tend to elect retirement at an earlier age than white-collar workers. Explanations for this consistent finding include the possibility that blue-collar jobs require heavy physical exertion and work under unpleasant conditions. Accordingly, efforts directed at encouraging blue-collar workers to postpone retirement might require changes in job content aimed at reducing physical demands or changes in work schedules permitting a shorter workday.

Personal Characteristics

Individual characteristics potentially associated with the timing of retirement include sex, race, education, and health.

Sex. Women tend to retire earlier than men. Note, however, that in the past women may have been concentrated in lower-level jobs. Also note that until very recently, pension benefits were adjusted downward for women to correct for women's longer life expectancy. While it seems premature to estimate the effects of recently legislated unisex pension benefits on women's retirement intentions, as women gain access to a wider range of job opportunities, managers should expect that the retirement patterns for men and women will converge.

Race. Race has not been found to be associated with patterns of early retirement. It is possible that race effects are masked by stronger effects of educational level and job status.

Education. Educational level appears to be negatively correlated with early retirement decisions. In other words, workers with less formal education tend to elect early retirement. It is quite likely that they retire earlier because they are clustered in more physically demanding and less intrinsically motivating jobs.

Health. Perceived health status is the individual characteristic most strongly associated with early retirement planning. In a comprehensive survey of retirement patterns among employees in the automobile industry, it was found that subjective perceptions of declining health were strongly associated with plans for early retirement. Similarly, studies of new social security beneficiaries have indicated that "failing health" is the major reason for retirement.

In Chapter 6, we pointed out that estimates of the disabling effects of various illnesses and injuries are frequently erroneous. In several instances, a tendency to overreact to non-job-related health problems led to organizational retirement recommendations for older workers who desired to continue working. Organizational efforts to improve the interpretation of health information coupled with special programs to accommodate employees who suffer from nondisabling health problems may greatly reduce the degree to which health problems lead to early retirement decisions.

Financial Situation

Perceptions of the adequacy of financial resources for maintaining an acceptable standard of retirement life appear to be of major importance in determining the timing of retirement. Interestingly, individuals with lower retirement incomes and low job levels are most likely to retire early or on time. On the other hand, home ownership and high current salaries are also associated with retirement intentions.

Perhaps the relationship between the perceived adequacy of postretirement income and decisions to retire early might best be described as an inverted U. Individuals in low-paid positions with modest pensions may consider the costs associated with continuing work (transportation, clothing, etc.) excessive relative to retiring on even a very modest social security and pension income. Individuals eligible for high pension benefits may similarly determine that it is economically unwise to postpone taking advantage of their anticipated financial well-being in retirement. Conversely, workers entitled to modest pension benefits to supplement their social security benefits may be most receptive to governmental and organizational incentives to postpone retirement.

Attitudes toward Work and Leisure

Research findings suggest that individuals planning to retire early get less satisfaction from their jobs and more satisfaction from their leisure activities. Workers who attach greater importance to work as a source of life satisfaction and are generally satisfied with their jobs are less likely to retire early. Accordingly, providing motivated senior employees with interesting and challenging work represents an important managerial strategy for influencing valued older workers to postpone their retirement plans.

Family Circumstances

The influence of family circumstances on retirement intentions has been examined in several studies. The findings suggest that working married women retire earlier than their male counterparts, timing their retirements to coincide with the retirement of their husbands. Moreover, the presence of a nonworking spouse in the home is associated with early retirement intentions for both male and female workers. The expectation of postretirement companionship from a nonworking spouse may encourage early retirement. On the other hand, the number of dependents is not associated with retirement intentions. In all likelihood, family circumstances interact with financial and health considerations in influencing the timing of retirement.

Community Circumstances

Very little is known about how various community factors influence retirement decisions. One investigator found a relationship between size of community and retirement intentions. Individuals living in large urban areas were more likely to postpone retirement than individuals living in small rural areas. It is not clear whether the greater availability of job opportunities for older workers in urban areas accounts for this difference.

More research is needed on the influence that various special services for older people, such as job banks listing postretirement opportunities, public transportation, and health maintenance facilities, have on retirement intentions.

In summary, health considerations and financial well-being have a strong and consistent influence on the timing of retirement. Sex and educational level also appear to affect retirement intentions. Government policymakers and organizational human resource managers must consider individual, family, and community variables as they develop incentives for encouraging both early and postponed retirement. In the next section, we examine the influence of government policies and economic considerations on the timing of retirement.

Effects of Government Policies

Returning to the retirement decision model depicted in Figure 8–1, we now consider the effects of government policies on retirement intentions. As we have previously noted, projections of an aging work force, mounting social security costs, and concerns about underutilization of human resources have stimulated new interest in public policies designed to give older employees greater opportunities and incentives to continue working. Here we consider the likely effects on retirement intentions of changes in the legislation governing mandatory retirement, inflation targets, and social security regulations.

Laws Restricting Mandatory Retirement

The first government policy factor in our model focuses on how retirement plans are influenced by legal restrictions on mandatory retirement. Sentiment is growing for the total abolition of a mandatory retirement age. The removal of age-based barriers to continued employment should enable older workers to enjoy greater flexibility in timing their retirement according to their own needs, desires, and circumstances. In future years, managers should anticipate that more senior employees will plan to retire at a later age under proposed government policies extending the minimum permissible mandatory retirement age beyond age 70 or completely abolishing a mandatory retirement age. Moreover, observing senior managers at work beyond age 70 is very likely to affect the views that younger workers have about the "appropriate" timing of their own retirement.

Inflation Rate Targets and Forecasts

The second government policy variable in the retirement decision model concerns the effects of inflation expectations on individual retirement intentions. Researchers have documented the importance of individual financial considerations in the retirement decision process.[1] For many prospective retirees, personal savings and anticipated income from private pension plans and social security benefits provide a baseline for estimating the adequacy of postretirement income. The accuracy of these financial projections, however, depends on future rates of inflation.

Retirees living on fixed incomes are particularly vulnerable to a significant deterioration of purchasing power resulting from high inflation rates. This means that greater numbers of senior workers will elect to continue working beyond the traditional retirement age of 65 during periods of high inflation. Which ones do so will depend on individual financial status. Workers in the lower and middle salary ranges are most likely to postpone their retirements during such periods.

Social Security Regulations

The third government policy variable in the retirement decision model concerns the effects of changes in social security regulations on retirement intentions. In recent years, concerns have been expressed about the long-term financial viability of the social security program. Changes in eligibility requirements, in the computation of cost-of-living increases, and in medicare coverage have been proposed. Clearly, expectations about changes in social security policies and regulations will significantly influence retirement plans, particularly among senior employees for whom social security benefits will be a significant source of postretirement income.

Recently, a number of modifications of the present social security regulations have been adopted. In the future, those who do not claim their benefits for some years after age 65 will receive a percentage increase in monthly payments based on years worked. In addition, the benefit withholding rate for those who draw benefits but continue to work has been reduced, removing some of the disincentive for continued employment between the ages of 65 and 72. Specifically, under recent modifications of the social security regulations, the implicit marginal tax rate has been reduced from 50 percent to 33 percent on earnings above the exempt amount. Managers should anticipate that further increases in the financial incentives for postponing retirement that have been built into the social

---

[1]Richard Barfield and James Morgan, *Early Retirement* (Ann Arbor: University of Michigan Survey Research Center, 1969); and A. Hall and T. R. Johnson, "The Determinants of Planned Retirement Age," *Industrial and Labor Relations Review* 33 (1980), pp. 241–53.

security system, coupled with reductions in the financial penalties for continuing to work and draw social security, will encourage senior employees in lower- and middle-income categories to continue working beyond age 65 or to seek some type of postretirement employment.

In summary, the enactment of public policies extending the mandatory retirement age or abolishing mandatory retirement entirely, along with modifications in the social security benefit schedules designed to provide greater financial incentives for postponing retirement beyond age 65, are likely to encourage many more senior employees to remain in the work force longer.

Effects of Organizational Policies

Returning again to Figure 8–1, we now examine the influence of organizational policies on the retirement intentions of senior employees. Of interest here is how retirement plans are influenced by career planning, development, and retraining programs designed to preserve the employability of senior workers. Also of interest is how various pension and benefit plans encourage or discourage continuing to work beyond age 65. We look at how organizational norms regarding the "appropriate age" for retirement affect retirement intentions and at how corporate retirement policies affect the timing of retirement. In this connection, we consider how flexible retirement options, including opportunities for part-time employment, phaseout, and job modification, affect retirement intentions. Each of the variables considered in this section is under the direct control of management and can be altered to encourage older employees toward early, "on time," or late retirement.

Career Planning, Development, and Retraining

The first organizational variable in our retirement decision model concerns the effects of career planning, development, and retraining on retirement intentions. In recent years, a great number of organizations have confined their career planning for older employees to preretirement planning programs. Often seen as an investment in employee goodwill or as a special fringe benefit for older workers, these programs are designed to help ease the transition from employment to retirement.

In one of our recent studies, we found that of three human resource management programs designed for older workers—job redesign, flexible retirement options, and preretirement counseling—preretirement counseling was evaluated by personnel managers as making the greatest overall contribution to organizational effectiveness. It was also rated as the least costly of the three programs and the least difficult to implement. These findings suggested that human resource managers placed less emphasis on preserving the employability of older workers and more emphasis on encouraging their "on-time" retirement.

However, there are signs of a shift from an emphasis on easing older workers out at age 65 to an emphasis on maintaining their skills and preserving their employability. As we have noted in previous chapters, managers and human resource planners must begin to experiment with comprehensive programs of career planning, career development, performance monitoring, and, when necessary, retraining to maintain the skills of senior workers.

Chapter 5 detailed the importance of career counseling and vocational guidance. Individual and group career counseling often expands job horizons and permits middle-aged and older workers to explore alternative career paths.

In industries marked by rapid technological change, senior workers frequently risk the rapid obsolescence of skills. For some senior workers, career planning leading to the pursuit of a second career may help circumvent technological obsolescence. For other senior workers, retraining may be required to preserve employability. According to Rosow and Zager:

> Companies should develop a planning perspective that will enable them to view their employees as human resources whose regular assessment, enrichment, renewal, and modernization will benefit all concerned.[2]

The costs of career planning, development, and retraining can be substantial. However, replacement costs for experienced senior employees are also likely to be quite high, particularly in engineering and related high-technology fields. Accordingly, corporate investments in upgrading the skills of middle-aged and older employees, may prove to be quite cost effective in the long run.

We would expect that in future years organizational policies will be more supportive of career management, development, and retraining. In such a climate, senior employees will be more valuable to the organization and will be motivated to delay retirement. This is more likely to happen in occupations where obsolescence is a major problem.

Pension and Benefit Policies

We next examine the effects of organizational pension and benefit policies on retirement intentions. In past years, pension and benefit policies have for the most part encouraged "on-time" or early retirement and dis-

---

[2]J. M. Rosow and R. Zager, "Work in America Institute's Recommendations Grapple with the Future of the Older Worker," *Personnel Administrator* 26, no. 10 (October 1981), pp. 47–54.

couraged the postponement of retirement beyond age 65. With many private pension plans, eligibility for benefits begins as early as age 55 for employees with 25 or more years of service. Moreover, companies frequently offer senior employees a variety of bonuses and incentives for electing early retirement. The net effect of these policies has been to encourage early retirement.

Pension and benefit policies have also contained several economic disincentives for extending work life beyond age 65. Under the Age Discrimination in Employment Act of 1978, organizations have no legal obligation to make pension contributions on behalf of employees who elect to continue working after age 65. However, the EEOC is presently working on new rules that will require employer pension contributions to continue for employees over age 65. When these employees retire and begin collecting pension benefits, their monthly pension income may not reflect their longer service, higher salaries, or later pension starting dates. Similarly, under current regulations, companies are allowed to reduce their contributions for medical, disability, and insurance benefits of employees over 65. These policies, followed by about half of all major employers according to a recent Peat, Marwick, Mitchell & Co. survey, provide short-run financial incentives for retiring early and significant financial disincentives for postponing retirement.

A surprising number of employees are confused about how their pension benefits are calculated. According to a *Wall Street Journal* article, many people who continue working assumed that when Congress raised the mandatory retirement age to 70, their pension benefits were automatically extended. Freezing pension contributions at age 65, which has been branded "as a windfall for many companies," had substantial financial consequences. The *Journal* article provides the following illustration:

> Assume that a company uses a formula based on 1 percent of the final five years' average pay, multiplied by the number of years of service. A person whose "final-average pay" at age 65 was $25,000, after 30 years of service, would be entitled to an annual pension of $7,500.
>
> What if he decides to work another five years? By age 70, with moderate cost-of-living salary increases, his new final average pay figure might be $35,000, now multiplied by 35 years of service. If he gets credit for the extra years he has worked, that would boost his pension to $12,250 for a 63 percent increase in his retirement benefits.[3]

Only about 1 percent of companies grant actuarial increases for employees who agree to wait until age 70 before collecting benefits that they could have taken at age 65. Given the employee's shorter life expectancy at age 70 and the company's ability to retain earnings on pension investments for an additional five years, questions have been raised about the

---

[3] J. Bettner, "Will Your Pension Work Past 65 if You Do?" *The Wall Street Journal*, April 5, 1982, p. 44.

fairness of freezing pension contributions and failing to adjust benefits. The net effect of these policies has been to provide an economic disincentive for postponed retirement.

Given the changing age composition of the work force, the time is right for management to experiment with new pension and benefit policies that are designed to encourage postponed retirement in much the same way that previous pension and benefit policies were designed to encourage early retirement. Among the more innovative developments in recent years has been the emergence of "cafeteria-style" benefit programs. Under a cafeteria-style plan, employees select from various combinations of benefits a package tailored to their individual needs. The cafeteria approach seems particularly well suited to accommodating the special pension and benefit needs of older workers. For example, this approach permits older workers to select a certain level of health insurance coverage to complement their medicare benefits and create a comprehensive health protection plan. Older workers will be more likely to postpone retirement beyond age 65 when employer contributions to pensions and to health and life insurance plans continue for employees who elect to work beyond age 65.

Organizational Norms

Streib and Schneider found that older workers were more likely to delay their retirement if they experienced work group support for doing so. Conversely, work group pressures to step aside were associated with decisions to retire early.[4]

Our research on the effects of age stereotypes, discussed in Chapter 3, suggests that organizational norms dictating early retirement may be manifested in more subtle ways than direct work group pressure. For example, managers who hold age stereotypes may be less willing to work out performance problems, to incur retraining or updating expenses, and to approve promotion when dealing with older workers than they would be if they were dealing with identically situated younger workers. Our research findings quite clearly demonstrated how age stereotypes contribute to an organizational climate that discourages continued employment opportunities for older employees.

Supportive or discouraging organizational norms probably have a strong, often unrecognized, effect on individual retirement intentions. Management's ability to develop supportive organizational norms encouraging older workers to consider working beyond age 65 will convey a

---

[4]G. F. Streib and C. J. Schneider, *Retirement in American Society: Impact and Process* (Ithaca, N.Y.: Cornell University Press, 1971).

clear message to middle-aged and younger workers, namely, that contributions of senior employees are recognized and welcomed.

Returning to Figure 8-1, we now examine the influence of organizational retirement policies on the retirement intentions of senior employees. Of interest here is how retirement intentions are affected by the availability of flexible retirement options, including opportunities for part-time employment, phaseout, and job modification.

Flexible Retirement Options

Evidence is mounting on the effects of flexible retirement options on the timing of retirement. Sheppard has noted that for most workers approaching retirement age, the only available options are full-time work or no work at all.[5] Gerontologists have called for greater flexibility in retirement options, reflecting individual differences in desires and capacities, to encourage delayed retirement.[6]

Experiments in other countries with programs designed to maintain the employability of older workers, including provisions for part-time employment, phased retirement, vocational retraining allowances, and job modification, could serve as a model for American business. Recent evidence suggests that retirement intentions are influenced by the availability of at least one type of flexible retirement option, transfer from full-time to part-time status. Doctors, Shkop, and Denning found that a large proportion of individuals who continue to work beyond age 65 do so on a part-time basis. Interest in working until age 70 or beyond may be a function of the expanded work opportunity provided by part-time employment.[7]

Research by Shkop focused directly on how the availability of various job modifications for older employees would lead them to extend their employment. Shkop used questionnaires and in-depth interviews to learn more about the problems of 190 managers and 203 blue-collar workers.

When no flexible options were available, a larger proportion of the managers (76 percent) than of the blue-collar workers (61 percent) indicated a desire to continue working beyond the age of pension eligibility. Surprisingly, when Shkop presented the participants with the possibility of job modification as an alternative to retirement, the gap between the managers and the blue-collar workers increased. Interview data revealed that the strenuous physical requirements of the blue-collar jobs were not seen as

[5]H. L. Sheppard, *Research and Development Strategy on Employment-Related Problems of Older Workers: Final Report* (Washington, D.C.: American Institutes for Research, 1978).

[6]James W. Walker and Harriet L. Lazer, *The End of Mandatory Retirement* (New York: John Wiley & Sons, 1978).

[7]S. I. Doctors, Y. Shkop, and K. Denning, "Placement Services for Senior Citizens," unpublished manuscript, University of Pittsburgh, 1979.

essentially altered even after job modification. Accordingly, the blue-collar workers did not view job modification as very helpful.

When given the option of moving from full-time to part-time employment, 64 percent of the blue-collar workers compared to only 49 percent of the managers indicated a desire to continue working on a full-time basis. The blue-collar workers cited the desire to maintain their full salary as a reason for their preference. Both the managers and the blue-collar workers indicated a desire for longer vacation periods should they elect to postpone their retirement dates. Interestingly, the blue-collar workers indicated an interest in shorter workdays so as to better cope with the physical demands of their jobs, while the managers preferred a full eight-hour workday so as to preserve the continuity of their activities.

When presented with the option of altering the content of their jobs, the managers were enthusiastic about a variety of changes, including switching to other jobs and modifying their present jobs to place greater emphasis on consulting or on mentoring younger employees. Fewer blue-collar workers were interested in changing job content. However, among those who wanted to do so, reducing physical demands, increasing responsibility, and shifting to special assignments were mentioned.

About 20 percent of the survey respondents stated that they would be willing to accept a lower-level job instead of total retirement. Among the 80 percent who were unwilling to accept a demotion, most were concerned with the adverse effect that the accompanying lower salary might have on pension benefits. Many of these respondents said that they would accept a lower-level position if their doing so would not adversely affect the calculation of their pension benefits. Others said that while they welcomed a reduction in responsibilities, they feared that a demotion might be misinterpreted by co-workers as the result of inadequate performance in their present positions.[8]

In summary, Shkop's research suggests that offering senior employees job modifications and more flexible retirement options would probably increase their desire to postpone retirement. However, given the differences in the reactions of managers and blue-collar workers, companies might be well advised to target modifications and options to specific job classifications. From a managerial perspective, offering senior employees the possibility of altering the content of their jobs or changing their work schedules could have several payoffs. The retention of highly skilled employees is more likely when job requirements are matched with individual capacities and desires to continue working. In addition, permitting major job modifications could launch senior employees on the equivalent of second careers while opening career paths for younger employees.

---

[8] Y. M. Shkop, "The Impact of Job Modification Options on Retirement Plans," *Industrial Relations* 21 (1982), pp. 261–67.

Special Opportunities

Thus it has been demonstrated that older employees view options to alter their work schedules or modify their jobs as great incentives to postpone retirement. It has also been demonstrated that when flexible options are available, managers will use these options when making decisions about their employees. Our own research shows that flexible retirement options enable managers to retain older workers who for reasons of health, performance, or personal shortcoming would otherwise be viewed as unemployable.

The purpose of our research was to assess the effects of flexible retirement policies on personnel decisions for employees who were nearing the customary retirement age of 65. We were interested in determining the extent to which flexible retirement policies, involving various options for reassignment or job redesign, serve to reduce the termination rates of older employees. We also wanted to ascertain managerial preferences among various flexible option alternatives. Our research hypotheses were:

1. Administrators are less likely to recommend termination under flexible retirement policies than under inflexible retirement policies. (Inflexible retirement policies require either termination or continuation in the present position. Flexible retirement policies provide the options of termination, continuation, transfer, job redesign, or part-time phaseout.)
2. Termination decisions are particularly likely when low-performance employees are being reviewed under inflexible retirement policies.

The participants were 97 personnel administrators whose names were drawn from the national listing of a professional association. Each participant received a personnel simulation "in-basket" consisting of requests from four employees to postpone their retirement date. Each of the retirement problems was written in two versions, with the worker's performance depicted as low in one version and as average in the other. In addition, the corporate retirement policy was manipulated in the following manner. Preceding the retirement decision problems in each participant's in-basket was a statement of the company policies relevant to the retirement decision process. Half of the participants received a flexible statement (see Figure 8–2). The other half received an inflexible statement. The statements were identical except that options C, D, and E were listed only in the flexible statement.

The most striking finding of our investigation was the impact of flexible retirement options on the continuation of older workers. In all four of the cases, a flexible retirement policy led to a higher rate of continuation. With respect to our hypothesis concerning the effects of performance lev-

---

FIGURE 8-2

Flexible Retirement Policy

Relevant company policies to keep in mind as you make your decisions.

1. *Slow growth.* After a period of rapid expansion, Acme Sporting Goods Company is now entering a period of relatively stable employment. During the next five years, the work force is expected to grow at an annual rate of 4 percent.
2. *Performance evaluation.* The company is committed to a gradual upgrading of work standards and a strong emphasis on performance evaluation. A systematic program of performance evaluation will be the basis for promotion and salary recommendations, downward transfers, retirement recommendations, and terminations.
3. *Retention, retirement, and termination.* The company retirement policy has been changed to comply with the 1978 legislation governing mandatory retirement. Under the new law, an employee may retire with full pension benefits at age 65 or continue working until age 70 providing his or her performance meets acceptable standards.

   Employees who wish to continue working beyond age 65 must notify the company in writing prior to their 65th birthday. Upon receipt of written notice, the Vice President for Personnel will review the employee's personal file, including performance evaluations, health records, and other relevant data.

Upon completion of the review process, the Vice President for Personnel will recommend one of the following options:

A. *Termination.* In instances where it is clear that the employee is not capable of meeting or exceeding organizational standards, termination with regular retirement benefits should be recommended.
B. *Continuation for one year.* In instances where the evidence clearly indicates that an employee is capable of meeting or exceeding all of the job demands, this option should be recommended. The employee will continue to receive all regular benefits but will not receive any further increase in retirement funding. Retirement payments will not begin until actual retirement.
C. *Job transfer.* In instances where there is some reasonable question regarding the employee's ability to meet all job demands but there is an indication that in some other position the employee can make a contribution to the organization, a job transfer should be recommended. Salary adjustments commensurate with the new position will be made.
D. *Job redesign.* In instances where an employee is unable to meet certain job requirements and where it is feasible and practical to redesign the job so that the employee can meet or exceed the demands of the redesigned job, this option should be recommended. Salary adjustments commensurate with the new position will be made.

FIGURE 8-2 *(continued)*

E. *Change to part-time status.* In instances where there is some reasonable question regarding the employee's ability to meet all of the job demands but where there is an indicaiton that the employee would be capable of making a contribution to the organization on a part-time basis, this option should be recommended. Salary adjustments commensurate with the new position will be made automatically.

els, our findings suggest that termination decisions for low performers are far less likely under flexible retirement policies (termination rate under 50 percent) than under inflexible retirement policies (85 percent termination rate). The reasons given to support termination recommendations focused on performance, personal shortcomings, and health.

The implication is clear. Personnel administrators perceived that one or more of the flexible retirement options would provide opportunities to retain an older worker who might otherwise be viewed an unemployable.

Of the flexible retirement options recommended by the respondents, transfer was the most popular option. Continuation in the present job for one year was also popular. A change to part-time status was not popular except in instances where an employee had to scale down his or her workweek because of health problems. Despite recent trends toward part-time work and job sharing, the respondents seldom recommended these options. Job redesign was also unpopular, particularly for employees in blue-collar positions requiring strenuous physical activity. It should be noted that job redesign may be seen as more costly and disruptive to normal operation than other flexible retirement options.

In summary, our findings suggest that the development and implementation of new kinds of flexible retirement options should significantly expand older workers' opportunities for productive employment. The implementation of various flexible options must depend on such considerations as the level of interchangeability and interdependence among the jobs in a given organization and the compensation and pension adjustments required under these options. Experimentation with specific options that fit unique corporate needs and constraints should be encouraged.[9]

[9]Benson Rosen, Thomas H. Jerdee, and Robert O. Lunn, "Retirement Policies and Management Decisions," *Aging and Work* 3, no. 4 (Fall 1980), pp. 239–46.

Corporate Examples

In recent years, a number of companies have experimented with innovative ways to support the continued employment of older workers. Here we look at some of their efforts and provide managers with a way to learn about specific programs in their industry and geographic region.

It has often been noted that a true commitment to changing corporate policies must begin at the top. At CBS, founder William Paley remained as chairman of the board until he was 81. He then carved out a role for himself as a director of the company, chairman of the executive committee, and consultant at an annual income of $200,000. Clearly, there may be considerable flexibility for accommodating senior employees who own a chunk of the company.

Engineering and construction firms often hire back retirees during heavy work periods or use experienced retirees on special projects. Professors are sometimes asked to offer selected courses and continue their participation in research projects after their formal retirement. And sales representatives forced into retirement by one company may continue their careers as employees of former competitors with more liberal retirement policies.

Some companies offer special accommodations to senior employees in the lower ranks. Chase Manhattan Bank, IBM, Standard Oil, and Travelers Insurance have launched programs to reemploy retirees of their respective companies. Among the approaches that these companies use to permit senior workers to continue after retirement are job sharing, part-time work, and job banks of retirees who can handle temporary assignments. Travelers has offered brush-up courses to smooth the transition back to work. All of these companies have reported that former retirees are among their most dedicated and dependable workers.

A Northampton, Massachusetts, firm recently initiated a program in which employees begin volunteer work while receiving full salary in their final year before retirement. At first, they volunteer one day a quarter. Gradually, they increase the time they devote to this work. Employees relish the opportunity to make a useful contribution that is likely to carry over into their retirement.

Labor unions have attempted to capitalize on the organizational skills of retired members. Many members of the United Auto Workers and of the American Federation of State, County, and Municipal Employees who were instrumental in establishing these unions are now retired. Union officials are trying to harness the experience, knowledge, and motivation of these retirees to lobbying efforts and organizing drives.

Experiments with more flexible retirement options in other countries could serve as a model for American companies. In Sweden, for example, a new government policy allows workers in the 60–65 age category to cut back gradually on their workweek. This flexible option, called partial-pension, allows workers to ease the transition from full-time employment to full-time retirement. The findings of Swedish researchers indicated that going suddenly from full-time employment to complete idleness created difficult adjustment problems. In the new programs, shorter workweeks during the transition from work to complete retirement permit individuals to pursue hobbies and leisure-time activities in preparation for total retirement. Some employees opt for a shorter workweek, while others prefer a shorter workday. Job sharing is used to make up for the lost time. The program is subsidized by the government, which pays up to 65 percent of the lost wages.

Given the variety of approaches to creating more flexible retirement options, managers may justifiably become concerned over what plan is best for their particular work setting. In order to help managers learn from the experiences, both positive and negative, of other organizations in their industry and geographic region, the Institute of Gerontology at the University of Michigan in cooperation with the U.S. Administration on Aging has established a National Older Workers Information System (NOWIS). NOWIS provides a computerized information file comprising examples of the flexible retirement and work modification programs that companies have implemented. The file contains brief summaries of corporate efforts at creating new work options for older workers. The programs described are in the following categories:

1. Part-time and temporary employment opportunities for pre- and postretirees.
2. Full-time employment and retraining efforts and special positions created especially for senior employees.
3. Job redesigns, including modified work schedules, job sharing, and physical redesigns of job content.
4. Training, refresher courses, and second-career assistance.
5. Transfers, job downgrading, and assistance for laid-off employees.
6. Phased retirement, sabbaticals, and transition programs.

A narrative describing details of over 170 programs and listing company contact persons to whom inquiries may be directed is now available. Interested managers should contact NOWIS for more details at:

NOWIS
Institute of Gerontology
The University of Michigan
300 North Ingalls
Ann Arbor, MI 48109

Encouraging Early Retirement

Thus far, we have focused almost exclusively on policies aimed at encouraging older workers to continue working beyond the traditional retirement age. In some circumstances, however, policies may be needed that will encourage early retirement. For example, when organizations encounter economic downturns, they may prefer to offer senior employees new options for early retirement rather than to lay off middle-aged employees with less seniority. Similarly, providing senior workers whose job performance has dropped below acceptable standards the option of retiring may be preferable to terminating them. Consider the following example.

Case of Peter Blynski

Deregulation has dramatically changed the insurance industry. In St. Louis, for example, a mid-sized insurance firm recently merged with a full-service financial investment company. The merger led to dramatic changes in job requirements throughout both companies. For no one were the changes more sweeping than for the insurance agents who worked out of the home office in St. Louis.

Peter Blynski had grown up in the insurance industry. He joined the insurance firm in 1953, working out of its Springfield, Illinois, office. In 1967, he was assigned to Jefferson City, Missouri. He was transferred to Columbia, Missouri, in 1975 and to headquarters in St. Louis in 1980. During his more than 30 years with the firm, Peter had been recognized as a steady producer whose annual policy dollar volume placed him in the top half of its agents in most years. In three of those years, he wrote policies in excess of $1 million and received letters of commendation from the corporate vice president.

Since the merger, however, Peter Blynski had been working under increased stress. His job title had been changed from insurance representative to investment adviser, and he had been required to market a wide variety of financial services, including estate planning and money management. The company now offered many products beyond life insurance, including tax-sheltered annuities, real estate trusts, tax-exempt bond funds, a variety of specialized mutual funds, and commodities futures. Peter had found it difficult to keep up with the variety of new products and services, despite the weekly workshops, seminars, and training sessions.

During the first year after the merger, Peter had fallen farther and farther behind in meeting his sales targets. Moreover, his wife had commented several times about how tense he appeared. She had urged him to get a medical exam, but he had refused and had told her not to worry, wisecracking that he was well insured. Finally, after considerable soul-searching, Peter Blynski thought seriously for the first time about the possibility of early retirement.

When Peter met with his boss and the vice president for personnel, he admitted candidly that until the past few months he had intended to continue working until age 65 or possibly longer. However, the job pressures and job changes of the past year had given him second thoughts. He recognized that his work had been slipping, and he did not want to just "get by" for the next few years.

Peter noted that his eligibility for full social security and pension benefits would not begin for 3 1/2 years. He then learned from the personnel vice president that under special circumstances the company offered senior employees lump-sum payments that they could take as a cash bonus or spread out over the years until they were eligible for full pension benefits. In addition, the company was prepared to continue Peter's life insurance and medical benefits at the same level. Peter Blynski knew that accepting early retirement represented a gamble against the possibility of rising inflation in future years. However, after much deliberation, he decided to accept the company's offer.

This case illustrates some of the approaches that organizations have developed to encourage early retirement. Among the more popular early retirement incentives offered by organizations are social security supplements, lump-sum bonuses, extended medical and life insurance, cost-of-living pension increases, and early full-benefit plans.

Supplementing Social Security

Employees who are dependent on social security benefits for a significant portion of their postretirement income are understandably reluctant to apply for reduced social security benefits prior to age 65. In order to help such employees maintain eligibility for full social security benefits, some organizations offer employees who elect early retirement an income supplement equal to the amount of the social security benefits that they will receive at age 65.

Cash Bonus

Another approach involves offering employees a cash bonus, sometimes in amounts equal to two or three years of salary (often with payments spread out over an extended time period), as an incentive for early retirement. Employees who could use the extra money to further their education, underwrite a small business venture, or just travel might find a cash incentive a strong inducement for early retirement. Employees who anticipate possible layoffs might also welcome an opportunity to take early retirement on these terms.

Insurance

Employees are often concerned about the added expenses of paying for fringe benefits formerly paid by the employer should they elect early retirement. In order to offset such concerns, some companies offer to pay for a package of benefits, including life and medical insurance, from the date of early retirement until the employee reaches age 65.

Pension COLA

Perhaps the biggest concern among employees contemplating early retirement is the fear that rising inflation rates will reduce the purchasing power of fixed-income pension benefits. In order to help retirees plan their financial futures with greater certainty, organizations may guarantee cost-of-living adjustments to pension benefits.

Full Benefits Early

As an inducement for early retirement, a few companies are experimenting with plans that permit retirement with full benefits as early as age 55 or 58 for certain categories of employees. Individuals who have worked for some minimum number of years are eligible to retire at a relatively early age and to receive benefits at a level equal to that of retirees at age 65.

Employers are also experimenting with educational subsidies and outplacement counseling to help older workers pursue second careers after electing early retirement.

Admittedly, these programs are expensive. From a corporate perspective, however, the programs have these compensating advantages: they open promotion channels; they weed out poor performers; and they pare down overstaffed departments.

Summary

At the start of this chapter, we described the dilemma of Tom Black, the bank branch manager who wanted to retain an experienced cashier who was planning to retire. Our systematic examination of the individual retirement decision process provides a basis for policy revision and action planning aimed at motivating the continued productive employment of older workers. At the legislative level, changes governing the minimum permissible mandatory retirement age and changes in social security eligibility provisions could create new opportunities and incentives for older workers to continue working. At the organizational level, the present patterns of early or on-time retirement could be modified substantially by changes in pension and health insurance policies, career planning, and development programs for older employees; by changes in the job structure and work schedules of older employees; and by greater flexibility in regard to phaseout and part-time assignments for older employees. In our bank example, this translates into policy changes permitting part-time employment, work-at-home arrangements, or partial job redesign, while maintaining pension and benefits at levels prorated on the basis of hours worked. For companies that implement such policies, the payback would be continued utilization of the experience, training, and commitment of senior employees.

At the start of this chapter, we also learned that bank manager Tom Black hoped to offer an early retirement package to a senior loan officer. As we have noted, a flexible retirement policy should provide managers with the options needed to encourage early retirement, when appropriate. Cash bonuses, social security supplements, and extended medical and life insurance benefits could provide a higher level of economic security for employees who for reasons of health, performance, or changing interests decide to retire early.

We would encourage companies to experiment with policy revisions designed to accommodate corporate needs and individual preferences for early, on-time, or postponed retirement. Such policies will take us a step closer to full and productive utilization of human resources.

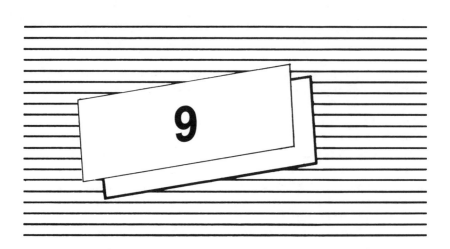

9

Working with Senior Employees

Main Issues

- Cross-generational relationships deserve special attention in management training programs.

- A first step is to identify the value differences of younger and older workers.

- Training should also include supervisory skills of confrontation, goal setting, and support.

- Attention should also be given to the problem-solving skills of both parties in mentoring relationships.

Moving beyond human resource management policy issues, we now consider the day-to-day problems that often occur when individuals in different age categories work closely together. Our goal is to highlight the kinds of communication problems, ambiguities, and conflicts that develop in cross-generational work relationships. For each difficulty, we suggest specific strategies to bridge the generation gap.

In recent years, organizations have given much attention to the integration of women and minorities into every level of the corporate hierarchy. Recognizing that stereotypes and prejudices can damage work relationships, companies offer seminars and workshops to promote harmonious relationships between the sexes and among racial and ethnic groups. Given the changing demographics of the work force, a good case can also be made for efforts to promote effective work relations between younger and older employees. The agenda for managerial seminars aimed at better relationships with senior employees might look like this example:

Managing Older Workers

Identifying value differences between younger and older workers.
Heightening awareness of age stereotypes.
Special problems between young managers and senior employees.
Problems between protégés and their mentors.

Identifying Value Differences between Younger and Older Workers.

Initially, the term *generation gap* referred to the differences in values, attitudes, and behaviors between parents and children. The same kinds of conflicts, misunderstandings, and problems that develop between parents and children may occasionally develop between younger and older workers.

Consider the values held by senior employees, who might be characterized as part of the postdepression generation. Many of these employees share a strong work ethic and place a premium on job and financial security. Some were first- or second-generation immigrants who still retained many customs from their homelands. They had their own standards of dress, listened to music unique to that era, and accepted principles of family solidarity, respect for authority figures, and patriotism.

Contrast the values of the postdepression generation of workers with the values of the workers who entered the labor force during the past decade. The younger workers may have grown up under more permissive child-rearing practices. Branded as the "me" generation, these workers place a high premium on the opportunity for self-actualizing work. Some of them reject their parents' aspirations to upward mobility and dedication to work in favor of a lifestyle that leaves ample time for the pursuit of leisure activities. A few have grown suspicious of big business and big government. Some took to the streets to demonstrate against or in favor of the Vietnam war. Many have experimented with drugs. This generation dressed in blue jeans, listened to hard rock, and adhered to the motto "Don't trust anyone over 30."

Given these large differences in attitudes, values, and lifestyles, the potential for occasional misunderstandings and communication breakdowns between younger and older workers is great. Older managers scratch their heads and puzzle over why the younger workers believe that the world owes them a living. Middle-aged workers battle mid-life crises and worry about discovering the meaning of life. Younger workers vow to avoid burnout and search for jobs that will let them do their own thing. Yet, to work effectively together, employees in these age categories must learn to appreciate each other's perspectives on work and life.

A frank discussion of the value differences of younger and older workers and how these differences are reflected in supervisory styles and expectations about worker loyalty, commitment, and career aspirations might be an effective way to begin a managerial workshop on improving work relationships among workers in different age categories.

Against this backdrop, the workshop participants might go on to examine several specific problems in the relationships between younger and older workers. The participants should explore the problems that arise when young managers supervise older workers. We have already noted in Chapters 2 and 3 the kinds of mistakes and mismanagement that can occur when young executives act on the basis of age stereotypes. Using cases, incidents, role playing and simulated decision exercises, participants of all ages can be alerted to how quickly and easily supervisors tend to fall back on age stereotypes in making a variety of day-to-day decisions. Next the workshop participants might consider the problems that occur when young managers withhold feedback or work around their senior employees.

Special Problems in Supervising Older Employees

Sociologists tell us that in interactions with another person, what we say and how we behave will vary quite a bit, depending on whether we have defined that person's status as higher than, the same as, or lower than our own. When all of the status cues are consistent, the appropriate behavior becomes obvious. For example, when a young management trainee meets an older, distinguished-looking man at a cocktail party and determines early in the conversation that his new acquaintance is an executive vice president with a major Dallas bank, the management trainee adjusts his behavior accordingly. He listens attentively, defers to the banker's opinions, and works hard to create a favorable impression of himself.

What would happen if the older-looking gentleman turned out to be a janitor? The management trainee might find this an awkward situation. The janitor would be accorded higher status based on his age and experience, but lower status based on the low prestige associated with his occupation. The cues regarding relative status would be inconsistent.

Younger managers often find it awkward to supervise older employees because of status inconsistencies. Role requirements often dictate that young managers plan, supervise, and evaluate the work of older workers. Yet providing feedback, particularly negative feedback, to an older subordinate can make a young manager uncomfortable. The problem increases in complexity when the older employee has many years of tenure and experience in the organization. And what if the manager is a young woman? The kinds of problems that often develop in status-inconsistent relationships between younger and older employees, illustrated in the following incident, should be considered thoroughly in the context of a management seminar. Perhaps even more important, thoughtful consideration should be given the question of how to handle sticky problems between young managers and senior employees more effectively in the future.

Case 1:   The Hart Bypass

At age 35, Joanna Hart's star was on the rise at Niagra Investments. After receiving her Ph.D. in economics from an Ivy League university, Hart moved to a staff position in the Treasury Department. Later she was appointed to serve on the Council of Economic Advisers. From her post in Washington, Hart assumed her present job as chief economist for Niagra.

Hart was the first female chief economist and the highest-ranked woman in the company. She recognized that her behavior would be watched closely. However, she felt that insights about power and politics gained in her previous positions would serve her well now.

Among her many responsibilities, Joanna Hart managed Niagra's advanced management training program. Niagra Investments placed a great deal of emphasis on in-house training for analysts and brokers. All new analysts and brokers spent five months in training, attending short courses on all aspects of economics, finance, and investments. Experienced brokers and outside experts taught these courses. It was considered a high honor to be assigned to the training faculty, and brokers selected to teach a course received a $7,500 bonus. Competition was often stiff for the teaching assignments. Brokers who received high student evaluations were invited to teach again the following year.

Frank Crandall, a 22-year veteran with Niagra, taught the advanced investments course. His course had been well received in past years, but complaints about his teaching effectiveness had recently come to Hart's attention. In the end-of-course evaluation, students had commented that Crandall had failed to cover the newer econometric forecasting models. Other unfavorable comments focused on his use of dated examples to illustrate economic principles.

Joanna Hart commented to her assistant that handling the complaints against Crandall could be as politically sensitive as any of the problems she had encountered in Washington. Hart learned that Crandall took great pride in his teaching. She was also aware that several other brokers very much wanted a chance to teach the advanced investments course. Hart guessed that Crandall could become defensive if she confronted him directly about his poor teaching ratings. Crandall had made many friends in Niagra over the years. The last thing Hart needed, she confided to her assistant, was a coalition of angry old-timers bucking her every decision. Yet she felt that it would be unconscionable to jeopardize the training of analysts and brokers in order to spare Frank Crandall's feelings.

After further deliberation, Hart devised an action plan. Rather than risk an argument over Crandall's teaching, she reassigned Crandall to an investor relations position. She stretched the truth a bit and told

Crandall that the recent proliferation of complex investment instruments had led to a deluge of calls and letters, creating an overload for the investor relations staff. She also hinted that this would be a temporary assignment.

Crandall accepted the reassignment at face value and moved into his new investor relations role. He found the work routine and unchallenging. His memos requesting a reappointment to the training faculty for the following year went unanswered for months. When a reply finally came through, it vaguely noted that his services were still needed in investor relations. Over time, Crandall grew discouraged. He took an unusually large number of sick days. The head of the investor relations section reported that Crandall had developed an apathetic attitude to customer inquiries.

Hart again puzzled over how to handle Crandall's deteriorating performance. She wanted very much to spare his feelings and avoid an unpleasant discussion. She wondered how a young woman and relative newcomer to the investment firm could convince a 22-year veteran to change his ways. Last month she recommended him for only a token merit increase. Apparently, he still had not received the message.

About 10 months later, Joanna Hart reassigned Crandall. This time, she sent him to a small satellite office in the suburbs. Again, the new chief economist felt that nothing positive would come out of a confrontation with Crandall. So she again explained the reassignment as a temporary measure until the office manager could properly train a new analyst.

Crandall grudgingly accepted the change. Ironically, his duties in the satellite office were about the same as those of many of his former students in the advanced investments course. Colleagues in the office noticed that over time he seemed to withdraw. He seldom conversed with others in the office. The office manager characterized him as a case of "borderline depression." Three months after his second reassignment, Frank Crandall called the corporate personnel office and requested immediate early retirement.

Analysis of Case 1

In the context of a management awareness workshop, reactions to the Hart Bypass case typically vary. Some of the younger participants agree with Hart's decision to avoid openly confronting Crandall with his negative teaching evaluations and his poor performance in the investment relations department. A few participants cite firsthand examples of communication barriers between young supervisors and experienced senior employees. In fact, workshop participants are very likely to argue that the case reached a satisfactory conclusion with Crandall's eventual voluntary early retirement.

Other participants take a different view, pointing out that Hart's unwillingness to confront Crandall set off a chain reaction of misunderstandings. They argue that by circumventing Crandall rather than directly confronting him, Hart escalated a minor performance problem to a point beyond reconciliation and that as a result the organization lost a valued senior employee unnecessarily.

There is no formula for resolving all of the misunderstandings that develop between young supervisors and older employees. We believe, however, that young managers can learn confrontation and problem-solving skills that will enable them to deal with the performance problems of older employees in a positive manner. Honest confrontations have two major advantages over more circumspect methods of dealing with older workers. One advantage is that senior employees have an opportunity to improve when a clear understanding of the problem is imparted to them. The other advantage is that honest feedback opens the possibility for joint creative problem solving by the manager and the employee.

Open confrontation of performance problems carries some real risks. At Niagra Investments, chief economist Hart felt that a confrontation with Crandall might have negative consequences. She feared that Crandall would react defensively to feedback from a younger manager and that other employees would resent her pulling rank on an experienced senior employee. Whether or not her concerns were justified would have depended on her skills in communication, confrontation, and problem solving. In the context of a workshop, young executives can develop confidence in their own abilities to deal constructively with performance problems encountered among senior subordinates. A good starting point would be the development of effective confrontation skills.

Confronting Poor Performers

Effective confrontations clearly and unambiguously communicate the nature of the poor performance, spell out the organizational consequences of unacceptable behavior, and give the poor performer flexibility in choosing how to improve. The components of an effective confrontation are shown in Figure 9-1. We examine each of these components in the context of Frank Crandall's performance problems.

Specific examples of ineffective or substandard behaviors carry much more information than do vague characterizations of the employee's motivation or personality. Telling Frank Crandall that his students want exposure to sophisticated econometric forecasting models communicates much more effectively than does telling Crandall that his teaching is deficient or

---

FIGURE 9-1

Effective Confrontation of Poor Performance

Clear statement of the problem in behavioral terms.
Organizational consequences of ineffective performance.
Choice of "acceptable" options for improving performance.

---

incompetent. Similarly, telling Crandall that he handled too few investor inquiries is preferable to labeling him apathetic.

Effective confrontation also requires managers to spell out the consequences of the substandard performance for the department or unit. In confronting Crandall with his low productivity in dealing with investor inquiries, for example, Hart could have stated, "When you handle only a few investor problems, the burden of answering the remaining calls falls unfairly on other brokers and drives up costs for maintaining good investor relations." A clear statement of the consequences of poor performance communicates the seriousness of the problem.

Effective confrontation allows the poor performer an opportunity to save face and make a commitment to improve. Open-ended statements identifying specific areas that need improvement are often superior to directives and orders about future behavior. For example, Hart might have used this open-ended statement: "I'm concerned that you are not covering econometric forecasting models in your investment course for analysts and brokers. This deprives our new brokers of learning important tools necessary for carrying out their job responsibilities." An open-ended confrontation shifts the burden for improvement directly to the ineffective performer. The message from the supervisor is one of trust that the subordinate will take the initiative and work toward improvement. The open-ended confrontation permits the subordinate to select from several alternatives a particular course of action that seems personally compatible.

Consider how Frank Crandall could have reacted to a direct, open confrontation regarding the omission of econometric forecasting models from his investment training course. Crandall might have agreed immediately to include the missing models. Or he might have volunteered to change teaching assignments. Or he might have requested a one-year leave of absence from teaching in order to brush up on econometric forecasting models. Whatever strategy Crandall selected for solving the performance problem, we would anticipate that he would be highly committed to it. Of course, Crandall's boss retains final approval over the course of action chosen. Hart has no obligation to go along with a plan that could create problems elsewhere in the organization.

Note that the philosophy underlying open confrontation differs markedly from the philosophy underlying a more circumspect approach to dealing with the performance problems of senior employees. The confrontation approach assumes that when senior employees learn of their substandard performance, they will make a good faith effort to improve. Managerial decisions to work around the performance problems of senior workers are frequently based on the philosophy that senior workers will be unwilling or unable to improve. Often this more pessimistic view of the reactions of older workers derives from age stereotypes.

In workshop settings, managers develop insights into a possible self-fulfilling prophecy effect in dealing with older workers. Young managers who are uncomfortable about providing negative feedback to senior employees often attempt to solve problems by working around them. They rationalize their actions on the basis of stereotypes that view older employees as resistant to change. The bypass route robs senior employees of the chance to overcome performance deficiencies. It also robs junior executives of the opportunity to practice and build confidence in their confrontational skills.

Case 2:   Pressure in Personnel

Joanna Hart was not the only young executive at Niagra Investments with problems in supervising a senior employee. Barry Alderman, who was in charge of Niagra's college recruiting, could not remember a more hectic time in his life. When Barry was promoted to head of college recruiting, Mr. Maketa had told him that the job would test the energy and endurance of even a fit 29-year-old former varsity tennis player. During the past two months, Barry had visited 24 universities on the East Coast and had interviewed more that 200 MBA students for entry-level investment adviser positions. The experience had been exhausting. Because of his road schedule, Barry had had to rely heavily on his administrative assistant, Betty Aluise, to handle many of the duties that he usually attended to personally.

Since returning to the office, Alderman had become increasingly aware of Betty Aluise's aloofness. He sensed that she was purposely avoiding him. He also noted that she quickly looked away when he questioned her about a late travel voucher or a missing applicant file. A little investigating revealed that Betty was behind in her routine responsibilities and was now over a week late with an important EEO/AA report. Betty's failure to attend a monthly staff meeting was the last straw for Alderman. He was determined to get her back on track or to find someone else who was capable of managing the workload. He left a note for Betty, requesting that she meet him in his office at 8:45 Monday morning.

Betty had been having her own doubts about her ability to manage the growing workload and about her future at Niagra Investments. Returning to full-time work four years ago at age 53 had represented quite a change for Betty. Although she had worked as an executive secretary before her marriage, her previous positions had been much less demanding than her present position.

At home, Jim Aluise had also noticed a recent change in his wife's behavior. She seemed tense and short-tempered. During a Saturday evening dinner at their favorite Italian restaurant, Aluise asked his wife about problems in the office. Over the antipasto, Betty confided that she thought her boss was subtly pressuring her to quit. She explained that Alderman had told her to complete several complex monthly EEO/AA reports without lessening her regular workload. While waiting for her minestrone to cool, Betty confessed to Jim that the reports required many statistical calculations. Some of the calculations were beyond anything she had ever encountered before. Completing the reports accurately seemed to take forever.

The waiter brought Betty's risotto with shrimp and a side order of finocchio au gratin. Betty told Jim how she had worked through lunch hours two and three times a week. She related how she had skipped staff meetings just to catch up on her regular paperwork. As her husband listened intently, Betty confessed to feeling both overwhelmed and incompetent. Finally, relaxing over espresso and biscuit tortoni, Betty said that with six more years to go before her retirement, she wondered why her boss wanted to force her out. Perhaps her future with the company would be resolved at the Monday morning meeting with Barry Alderman.

Analysis of Case 2

How Barry Alderman handles the Monday morning meeting with his administrative assistant will have a lasting effect on the ability of the two of them to work together in the future. We can easily envision a meeting at which Betty Aluise becomes increasingly frustrated, feels unfairly treated, and hands in her resignation. On the other hand, if Alderman uses effective problem-solving skills, his working relationship with Mrs. Aluise will improve and she will work more productively.

What Alderman needs for dealing with his administrative assistant is an approach that will minimize her defensiveness, capitalize on her experience and insights, and build commitment to resolve the problem. Behav-

FIGURE 9–2

The Problem-Solving Sequence

1. Problem identification
   Manager confronts senior employee with performance problem.
   Manager attempts to see situation from employee's perspective.
   Manager and employee agree on problem definition.
2. Brainstorming alternative solutions
   Manager and employee contribute ideas for solving problem.
   Evaluation of ideas is temporarily suspended to foster creativity.
3. Choice of mutually acceptable solution
   Manager and employee evaluate each alternative.
   Alternative that most effectively responds to problem definition is selected.
4. Solution implementation
   Manager and employee agree on how solution will be implemented.
   Timetable for implementation is set.
5. Evaluation of solution
   Manager and employee assess effectiveness of solution implementation.
   Ineffective solution stimulates redefinition of problem (begin sequence at
      step 1).
   Ineffective solution stimulates need for new alternative solutions
      (begin sequence at step 3).

ioral scientists have described approaches to problem solving that may be particularly applicable to the kinds of work-related problems encountered by young managers and senior employees.[1] The problem-solving process requires managers and employees to work through a sequence of steps from problem identification through evaluation of implemented solutions. The problem-solving sequence is shown in Figure 9–2.

In workshops concerned with the management of the senior employee, the participants can sharpen their problem-solving skills through case discussion, behavioral modeling, and role playing. Consider, for example, how Barry Alderman would follow the problem-solving sequence with Betty Aluise at their Monday morning meeting.

Alderman might begin the meeting by explaining his desire to utilize the problem-solving sequence. His goal is to reduce elements of threat and defensiveness in the discussion and assure his employee that the two of them will be working toward mutually acceptable solutions to their work

[1]See, for example, T. L. Gordon, *Leader Effectiveness Training* (New York: Wyden Books, 1977); R. Likert and J. G. Likert, *New Ways of Managing Conflict* (New York: McGraw-Hill, 1976); and N. R. F. Maier, *Problem-Solving Discussions and Conferences: Leadership Methods and Skills* (New York: McGraw-Hill, 1963).

problems. Accordingly, he begins with a statement along these lines: "Betty, I'm concerned about several problems, and I hope the two of us can work together to solve these problems." Note that Alderman's approach is nonblameful. He focuses on the need to solve problems, not on assumptions about who is to blame.

As shown in Figure 9–2, problem identification (step 1 in the problem-solving sequence) begins with the kind of open-ended confrontation that we have described earlier. Alderman says, "I'm worried about missing the EEO/AA report deadlines. Without those reports, I cannot complete my monthly recruiting reports on time. I'm also concerned that some of the routine paperwork has fallen behind. Delays in scheduling applicants for second interviews risk losing excellent prospects."

Alderman must now attempt to appreciate how his administrative assistant sees the situation. It is quite likely in this situation that Betty Aluise would tell Alderman that she had worked extra hours in order to catch up. Perhaps she would also reveal that computing complex statistical calculations has really slowed her down. Alderman may be surprised to learn that his assistant feels very insecure about her future.

Sharing perspectives on the problem openly and honestly helps clarify the underlying issues. As the meeting continues, we might expect the following dialogue:

Manager: My travel schedule has been hectic during the past few months. I need to delegate more of the office work while I'm on the road.

Assistant: I want to help you as much as possible, but I just can't manage the workload. Lately, I have felt overwhelmed by all of the extra work. Frankly, the statistical calculations are sometimes over my head.

Manager: I think I have a better understanding of the problem. The report deadlines are fixed. We can be a little more flexible about your other assignments, but they cannot be postponed very long either. Let's take a few minutes and consider our options. Can you see any way that we can meet our schedules without making your workload impossible?

(Alderman has set the stage for brainstorming alternative solutions, step 2 in the problem-solving sequence.)

Assistant: Perhaps we can hire a "temp" to handle some of the paperwork during your heavy travel period.

Manager: Let me make a note of that possibility. I'll try to make a note of each solution. Then we can go back and see which alternative seems most practical. Your idea made me think that we could look into reorganizing some of the work among our present staff. Perhaps someone in another department could come over to personnel and lend a hand.

Assistant: I've talked the problem over with my husband over the weekend. He thought there might be some computer programs that we could use to calculate our EEO statistics. I don't know much about computers, but maybe someone could write a program that could be reused each month. Over time, the cost of creating the program would be recovered by our greater efficiency.

Manager: We should look into the computer idea. I did not appreciate how much trouble the calculations were causing. Would you be interested in enrolling in a statistical refresher course? The company would take care of your tuition expense.

Assistant: I don't have much statistical aptitude. Given how far behind I am now, taking time to attend a refresher course would create more problems.

Manager: Well, we have come up with several good ideas for catching up. I suggest we meet again on Wednesday morning to decide how to handle the problem. In the meantime, we can gather more information about our proposed solutions. I will check on the availability of existing computer software and how much it would cost to have a program tailor-made for our EEO reports. Would you look into the costs of hiring a temporary employee for two months and find out whether we can borrow someone from another department to help us out?

Assistant: Sure, Mr. Alderman. Thanks for being so supportive. I didn't know what to expect this morning. Now I feel confident that we will solve this problem. No more missed deadlines or staff meetings, I promise.

At their Wednesday meeting, Alderman and Aluise should have at hand the information necessary to evaluate alternative solutions to the work overload problem. They will be at step 3 in Figure 9–2, the choice of a mutually acceptable solution.

During their discussion of the attractiveness and feasibility of alternative solutions, Alderman and Aluise ruled out two alternatives quickly. Betty Aluise reaffirmed her decision not to attend a refresher course in statistics. Examination of the personnel budget for the year revealed that adequate funds could not be found to hire a temporary employee for several months. Accordingly, Alderman and Aluise focused on the remaining alternatives in their discussion.

What emerged from this meeting surprised and satisfied both of them. A two-part plan of action was agreed upon. Beginning immediately, Alderman was to redistribute the assignments so that an employee with strong statistical skills would work on the quantitative portion of the EEO/AA reports. In return, Aluise was to write the narrative section of several new reports in addition to performing her other duties. Alderman and Aluise also agreed that they would purchase on approval several computer software programs. Their goal was to find a computer program that could handle the EEO monthly statistics.

Before the meeting ended, Alderman and Aluise agreed to meet again in two months for the purpose of evaluating the success of their plan. In the meantime, Barry Alderman made a mental note to check informally with Betty Aluise and other members of the personnel staff to ensure that workload assignments were fairly distributed.

Several weeks after the meeting, Betty and Jim Aluise were enjoying dinner in their favorite Chinese restaurant. Betty told Jim how much better she felt about her job. Over stir fried squid with scallions and ginger, Betty said that her anxieties about forced early retirement had been completely unfounded. By the time their dessert of Chinese pancakes with apricot filling and peanuts arrived, Betty had noted that her communication with Barry Alderman had improved immeasurably. In fact, she said that since he traveled so much, it might be nice to invite him over for a good home-cooked meal one evening.

In workshops concerned with managing the older worker, young managers like Joanna Hart and Barry Alderman can develop skills in confronting their senior employees about performance problems and in using effective problem-solving skills to resolve work-related conflicts. Practice in these skills should help young managers gain the courage to deal openly and directly with senior workers. The payoffs for open confrontation and problem solving frequently include reducing misunderstandings, making better decisions because of the inputs of senior workers, gaining strong commitment for the implementation of mutually agreed-upon decisions, and building more trusting work relationships with senior employees. Occasionally, the young managers may reap the fringe benefit of a home-cooked meal.

Problems between Protégés and Their Mentors

A full-fledged workshop on work relations between younger and older employees should include consideration of the problems that are often encountered between senior mentors and their young protégés. A few organizations have created formal policies governing the development of young managers. Newcomers to these organizations are assigned to senior mentors who are charged with the responsibility for coaching and counseling them. In other organizations, the mentoring process evolves informally, based on common interests between senior managers and young people who aspire to climb the corporate ladder.

From the young protégé's perspective, much can be gained from a mentor relationship. The opportunity to observe a senior manager in action and to have a source of advice, counsel, and even entrée to influential others in the organization can be a powerful force for career advancement. Moreover, the give-and-take between the mentor and the protégé contributes immensely to the young manager's self-confidence.

What's in it for the mentor? From the perspective of the senior employee, the opportunity to influence the career of an aspiring young manager can be a very rewarding experience. Knowing that they have had a part in preparing future generations of managers to carry out complex, challenging responsibilities vital to the organization's future effectiveness carries its own intrinsic reward for mentors. Often mentors report that the stimulation provided by young employees contributes to their own growth and vitality.

Mentor-protégé relationships have many parallels to parent-child relationships. As parents and children will readily testify, these relationships are not without problems. Struggles to gain independence from an overprotective mentor can pose some real conflicts for the young manager, as illustrated in the following case.

Case 3: The Captain

Marine Corps captain, former all-American football player, and world traveler, at age 58 Conrad Lucas is almost a living legend among his colleagues in a major Wall Street brokerage house. Since joining the firm in 1969, Lucas has advanced rapidly through the ranks, working his way up to his current position of senior partner. During his rapid rise to the executive suite, he gained a reputation as an innovator. He created the concept of real estate limited partnerships for the small investor. He also championed the reorganization and expansion of his firm into autonomous functional divisions.

In recent years, Conrad Lucas has dedicated himself to grooming junior account executives for higher-level management positions. Identifying talented people early in their careers and coaching them informally provides Lucas with an opportunity to shape the firm's future leaders. Among some junior managers, Lucas is known as the quintessential mentor. Among a few others, he is known as "The Captain," because of his Marine Corps philosophy that you need to break down a person's identity before you can mold it properly.

Over the years, Lucas' mentoring has taken many forms. He has offered some junior managers invaluable career advice. His ability to provide informal counseling and his sound knowledge of the political infrastructure of the firm have helped many young managers avoid fatal career mistakes. On occasion, he has dropped the name of a protégé during important deliberations of the personnel committee. It's no secret that his protégés advance far and fast.

While most of the firm's junior account executives would give up their spa memberships, their company expense accounts, and their underground parking spaces for an opportunity to work with Conrad Lucas, for one account executive, Bill Kesner, the price of being a Lucas protégé is just too high. Bill values the informal counseling that Lucas provides, the insights that Lucas offers about which partners have the power to make things happen, and the possibility that Lucas will mention his name during promotion committee meetings. However, Bill has never been comfortable with the blind loyalty that Conrad Lucas demands from his protégés.

Although Lucas and Kesner have worked well together for several years on different projects, recently they have been far apart on many key investment issues. Kesner learned early in their work relationship that Conrad Lucas viewed disagreement as disloyalty and close to insubordination. The conflict for Kesner is between his indebtedness for all that Conrad Lucas has done to help his career, and his desire to break off the mentor relationship and assert his own identity in the firm. Further complicating the situation, Kesner has heard rumors that in the past, when protégés have asserted themselves with Conrad Lucas, he has become furious and had branded them as ingrates. Not so coincidentally, these rebellious junior executives have often found that their careers have careened off the fast track, often coming to a screeching halt.

Kesner commented to his wife that severing his ties to Lucas was harder than convincing his own father to trust him with the family car for the first time. That same desire for independence from the ties of a strong authority figure seemed to be operating in his work relationship with Conrad Lucas. Kesner wondered out loud why senior executives like Conrad Lucas could not "let go."

Analysis of Case 3

How can young executives like Bill Kesner who are caught in this type of double bind free themselves from the mentor-protégé relationship?

In many instances, the mentor-protégé relationship breaks off naturally. After anywhere from 3 to 10 years, the protégé moves on to another role (and not infrequently to another mentor). In other instances, the mentor retires or dies. However, in a few instances, such as the one illustrated in the preceding case, there appears to be no happy parting of the ways.

While most mentors are motivated by the desire to promote the best interests of their young protégés, even mentors with the best of intentions may have destructive effects on young managers. The effects parallel the self-doubt and inferiority that are fostered by a well-meaning but overprotective parent. And when a mentor fears that his own accomplishments will be overshadowed by those of his protégé, he may smother initiative and creativity. In extreme instances, mentors become critical, demanding, and even tyrannical in their insistence on total loyalty and dedication.

In his relationship with "The Captain," Kesner's intense conflict derives from the conflict between his feelings of respect, admiration, and gratitude, on the one hand, and, on the other hand, his feelings of resentment and intimidation and his desires for independence and autonomy. Often such conflicts lead to communication breakdowns, avoidance, and withdrawal. Yet guilt feelings often linger long after the mentor-protégé relationship has dissolved.

Note the similarities between the interpersonal bypass described earlier in this chapter, where a young manager avoids confronting a senior employee, and the avoidance reaction to resolving problems in the mentor-protégé relationship. While the latter situation is much more complex, the same kinds of confrontational and problem-solving skills that were recommended in the earlier case may prove quite useful in dealing with it. In the context of a workshop focusing on work relationships with senior employees, frank discussion should be encouraged about the benefits of mentor-protégé relationships and about effective strategies for coping with the occasional problems that are encountered in these relationships.

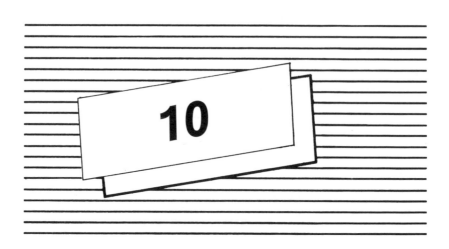

Putting It All Together:
Organizational Strategies

In this chapter, we shall discuss strategies that organizations can follow for the management of older employees. These strategies range from a minimal effort, involving only legal compliance, to an all-out effort to be a leader in the management of older employees. We shall point out the major pros and cons of each strategy. Where should an organization position itself with regard to these strategies? This depends on the basic values of the organization, the organization's competitive environment, the organization's work requirements, and the composition of the organization's work force.

Obviously, our own viewpoint is that most organizations can benefit from greater efforts to help older employees maintain their employability. Accordingly, we shall devote our greatest attention to "putting it all together" into one coherent maximum-effort strategy drawing on all of the policies and procedures discussed in previous chapters. We shall, however, try to present a balanced picture of the costs and benefits of various strategies, recognizing that managers must often make difficult trade-offs and compromises for the good of the whole organization.

In earlier chapters, we have described actual company practices. Many of the organizations mentioned stand out as leaders in one or more particular activities, but very few are able to stand out as leaders across the board. Please bear in mind that the strategic categories presented in this chapter were developed by the authors for the sake of clarity and simplicity of exposition. We certainly do not mean to suggest that any one organization should attempt to position all aspects of its program for older employees entirely within one of the strategic categories.

Another preliminary point deserves special emphasis. Strategies must be dynamic, changing in response to the external and internal environments. In the areas of human resource management and labor relations, steady state strategies seldom succeed for long. Companies cited as models one day may find themselves cited as pariahs the next. Furthermore, even the strategically alert organization with the best of values, intentions, and policies can expect to stumble just a bit here and there along its strategic path for the management of older employees.

Three basic strategies for managing older employees will be discussed. The *elimination* strategy, which we will examine first, concentrates on forcing or enticing older employees to leave the organization. The *neutral* strategy takes no particular stance toward older employees except as required by law. The *retention* strategy aims at keeping older employees on the job for as long as they are willing and able to continue.

Elimination Strategy

It may be unfair to characterize any organization as having a strategy of deliberately eliminating older employees to the greatest extent possible. Some organizations, however, have adopted policies and procedures having that effect. The major ingredients of such a strategy are mandatory retirement at a specific age, special "buyout" incentives for early retirement, a retirement counseling program that encourages early or on-time retirement, and the withholding of developmental opportunities for older employees. In the elimination strategy there is also a complete lack of any attempt to provide special work arrangements that would enable older employees to extend their careers.

Mandatory Retirement

In 1984, mandatory retirement at a specific age was still the policy of many organizations, including many colleges and universities. Advocates of mandatory retirement at a specific age argue that this is necessary to clear out the "deadwood" and make way for the recruitment and promotion of "new blood." They argue that the odds favor improved performance through the replacement of old blood with new, even though there may be occasional exceptions. They argue further that even if they had the capability of judging each individual independently of age, doing so would be too hurtful to those older employees who would be judged unfit to continue. This argument has some merit, but it loses force when we consider the possibility of combining thorough and fair assessment procedures with enlightened programs for job change and job counseling.

Much more could be said here about mandatory retirement, but in view of current trends there may be little reason to say it. Outright policies of mandatory retirement at any specific age seem destined for the moral and legal scrap heap.

Buyout

Of greater interest currently is the notion of the "buyout," or offering special incentives for employees to retire early. Unlike mandatory retirement before age 70, special incentives for early retirement are permissible under current law. Such incentives have become quite popular in recent years, being favored by organizations that have found themselves overstaffed in periods of declining revenues. The idea behind these incentives is not so much to eliminate low producers as to reduce the financial burden of carrying large numbers of highly paid senior employees. Buyout incentives appeal to workers who are burned out, bored, tired, or anxious to pursue a new career. Buyout provisions have become quite popular in union contracts. They have also become a last resort for university administrations whose penchant for mandatory retirement has been thwarted by federal legislation.

To the extent that special incentives for early retirement allow the individual employee the option of continuing to work, they seem to be a defensible way to implement a strategy of eliminating older employees. The employee can judge for herself or himself the trade-offs involved and can come to a decision perceived to be in her or his own best interests. Similarly, the employer can also make a calculation of how much it is worth to get rid of the older employee and can set up the incentive system accordingly.

An obvious problem with this approach is that it assumes a mutuality of interests between employer and employee. It assumes that the bait will be taken by expendable employees and eschewed by employees whom the employer would like to keep, when in fact the reverse is often quite likely to happen. After all, the most competent older employees are often those who have the greatest opportunities for reemployment or alternative careers, so they may be quicker to take the bait.

The buyout approach is less likely to be successful in times of rapid inflation, unless appropriate protections are included in the incentive package. It is also less likely to be successful in situations where employees obtain substantial intrinsic rewards from their work. University faculty members have been known to refuse substantial monetary incentives in order to preserve their academic lifestyle. In some instances, it is almost as if they see acceptance of a buyout offer as selling out on their profession.

Other Ways to Grease the Skids

While mandatory retirement and buyout schemes may be the most obvious elements in a dumping strategy, there are other, more subtle components as well. One such component can be a retirement counseling or pre-retirement planning program. While such programs can be used as vehicles to persuade employees to postpone retirement, they are in fact often used, whether intentionally or unwittingly, as vehicles for skidding employees smoothly onto the retirement scrap heap. Which direction they lead depends almost entirely on the content of the programs, which in turn depends on management's goals in establishing them.

A dumping strategy may have other components, such as calculated changes in work assignments or in work environments, withdrawal of status symbols or perquisites, no longer seeking advice from the older employee, leaving the older employee out of luncheon invitations and golf games, and various other crudities. Not only are such devices distasteful, but they can end up enmeshing the perpetrators in an age discrimination suit.

In summary, various tactics are available to organizations that wish to pursue the strategy of eliminating older employees to the greatest extent possible under the law. These tactics vary in efficacy and in ethical acceptability, with buyout and counseling approaches getting the higher marks.

The elimination strategy is not likely to get an organization into serious difficulty unless it is pursued with such vigor that the organization ends up in court. There is also some risk of getting caught shorthanded in times of labor shortage (many are predicting a labor shortage for the coming decade). From a managerial viewpoint, a great advantage of the elimination strategy is that errors made in dumping potentially valuable employees tend to be invisible. When an organization needlessly retires a senior employee who would have made great contributions to the organization if allowed to continue, that error goes completely undetected. So here we have a relatively safe strategy. The costs, even when they are high, remain hidden.

Another advantage of the elimination strategy is its ease of administration. Mandatory retirement programs require little administrative attention from managers. Buyout programs, once established, are virtually self-administering from a managerial standpoint. The same goes for preretirement counseling programs, which can easily be farmed out to consultants.

The foregoing are genuine advantages of the elimination strategy, and they can be very appealing to busy managers. Do not, however, overlook the costs of the strategy: dollars spent on buyout and pension payments, lethargy among employees nearing retirement age, opportunity costs of poor career planning and development, and perhaps most important of all, employee indifference toward the organization.

Neutral Strategy

This strategy adopts no particular stance toward older employees except as required by law. The neutral organization does not go out of its way in either direction: it does not deliberately encourage or discourage retirement at any particular age, and it does not provide any special quarter for those employees who would like to continue beyond the traditional retirement age.

A neutral strategy is frequently characteristic of mature, steady state organizations such as public utilities and some government agencies. When an organization is known for pleasant and stable working conditions and a favorable pension system, and when recruiting and selection systems are quite highly developed and routinized, as is often the case with civil service operations, the retention of older employees is not likely to be a high-priority item for managers. Understandably, managers in such organizations may take a laissez-faire view, letting the employee decide what to do.

On the surface, a strategy of neutrality might appear to be quite defensible, if not downright desirable. After all, it allows the employee to continue if he or she wishes to do so, and it does not pressure employees into continuing when it is not in their long-term best interests to do so. It tends to have the same advantages and disadvantages as the elimination strategy, except that it is less hardhearted and therefore more acceptable to employees.

There is, however, a serious limitation to the strategy of neutrality. True neutrality is hard to come by. Neutrality is in the eye of the beholder, and an employer stance that is intended to be neutral may in fact be perceived by employees as quite unsupportive.

Retention Strategy

The retention strategy is aimed at retaining older employees as long as possible. It is based on the premise that maintaining the employment of older employees is good for organizations, for society, and for the older employees themselves.

Retaining older employees is seen as good for organizations because it lowers pension costs, lowers turnover rates and hence turnover costs, provides longer and larger paybacks for investments in training, contributes to high employee morale, and enhances the organization's reputation in the community.

Retaining older employees is seen as good for society because it lowers social security costs, adds to GNP and the tax base, and contributes to the social integration of the elderly population.

The retention strategy is seen as good for the older employees themselves because it keeps them physically and mentally active, maintains or enhances their self-respect, provides them with income, and satisfies their social needs by keeping them in daily touch with other active people.

Implementing a Retention Strategy

What can an organization do to implement a strategy of retaining older employees? The various approaches have been presented in considerable detail in previous chapters of this book. Here we shall emphasize, not the fine details of implementation, but the larger issues of generating the organizational will to adopt a retention strategy, setting specific goals for assisting older employees, gaining commitment to these goals, working out procedures and timetables for implementation, and making sure that action is taken.

Generating the Organizational Will.   Adopting a strategy and generating the organizational will to carry it out are two different things. Anyone in authority can make a pronouncement about assisting older employees, but that doesn't mean that anything will happen to carry it out. We know of one instance in which a large organization developed an elaborate affirmative action program and took great pains to publicize it internally and externally. In spite of these efforts, one year after the fanfare the manager of a major division stated flatly in an interview that the organization did not have an affirmative action plan or program. Problems of this sort are particularly prevalent in the area of human resource management. Policies fall flat unless they are accompanied by the organizational will to implement them.

How can managers generate the will to implement a policy of retaining older employees? In spite of what we have just said, the first step is a pronouncement from top management, along the following lines:

Policy on Older Employees

The policy of this organization is to encourage the continuing development and utilization of the talents of all employees, regardless of age, commensurate with employee abilities and desires. This policy is to be observed in all personnel actions, including human resource planning, staffing, performance assessment, career planning and development, job design, work assignment and scheduling, and retirement planning. Employees are encouraged to continue their employment as long as they are willing and able to do so. Managers at all levels are expected to provide flexible work arrangements and personal support in order to implement this policy.

The responsibility for observing this policy rests with all managers in the organization. Specific responsibility for coordinating, assisting, and monitoring observance of this policy is assigned to a task force consisting of the following persons.

The precise wording of such a policy statement is less important than the means by which it is created. If it springs from just one person or one department, its impact may be small. If it has the imprimatur of several major power centers within the organization, its impact will be much greater. Therefore, the policy statement should be the product of an ad hoc group consisting of top managers strategically located in the organization. The policy should be approved by the executive committee and the board of directors.

The task force responsible for implementing the policy must study carefully what needs to be done. If possible, a member of the task force knowledgeable in the specialized activities of personnel administration should develop a knowledge center relevant to personnel administration for older employees. Assistance from a knowledgeable consultant may be desirable at this point. The consultant's expertise should not be limited to preretirement counseling.

Persons with vested interests in current personnel policies and procedures should be on the task force. Persons in key positions on matters such as pension systems, job design, and work scheduling should also be included. If major responsibility for implementing the older worker policy resides in the personnel department, great care should be taken to include on the task force participants in key roles in operating departments. These are the people who will have to make the policy work on the firing line.

In the early stages of program development, the task force should take great pains to consult widely within the organization. Much of this activity may take place in meetings containing "consciousness raising" and "educational" components.

Don't forget to include at least several older employees!

Perhaps the most important step in generating organizational will is to make sure that reward contingencies support the policy. Managers should know that the age composition and individual career plans of their employees will be systematically monitored. Such monitoring should include interviews with employees who are opting for retirement. These interviews should explore retirees' perceptions of the degree of opportunity and support for continued employment that they received.

Setting Specific Strategic Goals.   Specific goals for the retention of employees in various age categories should be established by the task force. These goals should then be coordinated with operating managers at the level of the individual employee. There should be little room for surprises.

In other words, the career plans of all older employees should include plans for phasing into retirement. These plans should be on record in each department, and they should be aggregated by the task force and compared with program goals. The reasons for discrepancies should be explored, and either the goals should be brought into line with reality, or employees should be encouraged to modify their plans. Strategic goals should also encompass training and development activities, as discussed in more detail in Chapter 7.

Gaining Commitment to Goals. If the aforementioned planning activities are carried out in the recommended fashion, with broad participation of managers and older employees throughout the organization, commitment should follow. Commitment can also be strengthened by celebrating and publicizing the achievements and contributions of older workers within the organization. For most organizations, this would represent a shift away from celebrating retirements and toward celebrating continued contributions.

Working Out Procedures and Timetables. In order to make sure that the job gets done, specific procedures and timetables are needed. A system must be established for getting reports on the career plans of each older employee, including plans for development, job or schedule changes, and gradual retirement. A system must also be established for tying in these reports with the total human resource planning and development program.

Making Sure That Action Is Taken. The key here is to monitor the results of the program in terms of the development activities, career plans, and retirement decisions of older employees. These should be monitored and reported on a unit, departmental, and divisional basis, so that the effects of the whole effort are made visible. If effects are not in line with hopes, the reasons for discrepancies should be unearthed and dealt with.

What the Individual Can Do

Our discussion so far in this chapter has focused on installing a program for older employees at the organizational level. Many readers of this book will be looking for ways to take action at the level of a smaller unit within the organization. Whatever is done at the unit level must of course be congruent with general organizational policies and practices. This is an important limitation if you are in an organization that has a policy of mandatory retirement or other policies discouraging continuation past a certain age. In almost any organization, however, you can lend a hand to the older employee by encouraging career planning and development activities within whatever constraints are established by the organization.

Other important actions at the individual level include the supervisory skills of honest, thoughtful, and supportive confrontation discussed in detail in Chapter 9. Beyond these skills is the expression of your genuine respect for the older employee and the value that you attach to the past, current, and future contributions of the older employee to the organization and to your own development.

Guidelines for Change

Throughout our discussion, we have identified a variety of policies and practices that management can adopt in order to utilize fully the talents, experience, and commitment of senior employees. Our approach stresses early intervention to prevent serious problems of underutilization and obsolescence from developing. Here is a brief recap of the actions we recommend.

Action Components

1. Development of short- and long-range human resource plans to identify future demands and supplies for various mixes of skills, abilities, and experience.
2. Implementation of a comprehensive career-long program of career planning, guidance, and counseling. Integration of human resource plans with individual career goals to provide employees of all ages with a realistic picture of future career opportunities.
3. Systematic assessment of performance and health, with training for managers in performance assessment and feedback.
4. Design of organization-wide programs to combat obsolescence by maintaining employee skills and knowledge and by preparing employees for future change.

5. Creation of retirement policies that permit both corporate and individual flexibility. Flexible retirement policies should provide opportunities for employees to continue full time if they wish, to work part time, or to move into new roles compatible with their experience, interests, and capacities. Flexible policies should also remove rigid financial disincentives for continuing beyond the traditional retirement age, while continuing to provide financial incentives for early retirement when that is warranted.

The preceding are the major action components of a program for older employees. We have also advocated organizational efforts to create a climate supportive of the foregoing components but going beyond them to include day-to-day relationships on the job. We recommend the following to build this supportive climate.

1. Familiarizing managerial personnel with the legal considerations governing the employment of older workers. Managers at every level should be thoroughly conversant with the Age Discrimination in Employment Act and with its amendments pertaining to the extension of the minimum permissible mandatory retirement age.
2. Heightening managerial awareness of the pervasive influence of age stereotypes on day-to-day managerial decisions. Helping managers to overcome deep-rooted assumptions and expectations about the characteristics and limitations of senior employees.
3. Exploring value differences between older and younger workers. Providing skills in confrontation and problem solving to bridge communication gaps between young managers and senior employees. Examining special problems in the mentor-protégé relationship.

Admittedly, our recommendations constitute a full agenda for managers. Carrying out these recommendations, revising human resource management policies, and conducting managerial workshops on the problems of senior workers cannot be accomplished quickly or easily. There are trade-offs to be made between building a climate supportive of senior employees and devoting resources to other organizational priorities. For organizations that are ready to make a total commitment to the full utilization of older workers, we hope that the recommendations and examples set forth in this book will provide guidance and assistance in getting started.

Index of Cases by Topic

Age discrimination
  Avco Corp., 69
  Bishop v. Jelleff Associates, 63
  Carlton Jennings, 69
  Consolidated Edison Co., 57, 69
  General Motors, 58
  Greyhound Lines, 64
  Harlow Industries, 65
  Hodgson v. Tamiami Trail Tours, 64
  Houghton v. McDonnell Douglas, 65
  Ice Cream Company, 61
  INSKO, 60
  Liggett & Meyers, 58
  Mistretta v. Sandia Corporation, 68
  Pan American Airways, 57
  Rodriguez v. Taylor, 57
  Sales Representative, 69
  Standard Oil of California, 57
  Transamerica Motors, 63
  United Airlines, 58
  Wilsons Department Store, 69

Age stereotyping
  Carl Adams (sales management), 13
  Lawrence Evans (promotion), 44
  Ralph Adams (attendance at production
    seminar), 41
  Tedious Old Fool (handling customer
    complaints), 39
Career maintenance and development
  Hart Bypass, 168
  Pressure in Personnel, 172
  Retraining and Retaining, 88
  Too Young to Retire, Too Old to Manage,
    102
Corporate program
  Multitech, 131
Early retirement
  Paul Stanley, 4
  Peter Blynski, 160
Mentoring relationship
  The Captain, 178

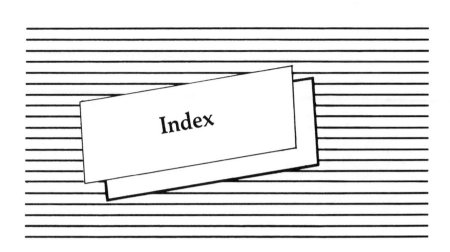

Index

A

Absenteeism of older workers, 27
Action components of program for older
    workers, 192
ADEA; *see* Age Discrimination in Employ-
    ment Act
Administration on Aging, viii
Age discrimination
    air traffic controllers, 65
    avoiding litigation, 75
    bona fide occupational qualification, 62
    burden of proof, 56
    bus drivers, 63
    business necessity, 56
    complaint (example), 73
    costs of litigation, 57–58
    firefighters, 64
    flight attendants, 63
    in help wanted ads, 60
    increased litigation, 57
    penalties, 57
    police, 64
    prima facie case, 56
    in promotion, 69–75
    in recruitment, 60
    in retention, 65–69
    in selection, 61–65
    senior scientists, 65–69
    test pilots, 65

Age discrimination—*Cont.*
    types of, 58–59
Age discrimination cases
    Avco Corp., 69
    Bishop v. Jelleff Associates, 63
    Carlton Jennings, 69–75
    Consolidated Edison Co., 57, 69
    General Motors, 58
    Greyhound Lines, 64
    Harlow Industries, 65–69
    Hodgson v. Tamiami Trail Tours, 64
    Houghton v. McDonnell Douglas, 65
    ice cream company, 61
    INSKO, 60–61
    Laugesen v. Anaconda Co., 68
    Liggett & Myers, 58
    Mistretta v. Sandia Corporation, 68
    Pan American Airways, 57
    Rodriguez v. Taylor, 57
    sales representative, 69–75
    Standard Oil of California, 57, 68–69
    Transamerica Motors, 63
    United Airlines, 58
    Wilsons Department Store, 69–75
Age Discrimination in Employment Act, 10,
    54–80
    amendments, 77–80
        effects of, 78–80
        coverage, 54

Age Discrimination in Employment Act—
  Cont.
  amendments—*Cont.*
    enforcement, 56
    exceptions, 55–56
    litigation procedures, 56–57
    penalties, 57
Age stereotypes, 14–33
  accuracy, 22
  effects on decisions, 34–50
  ego defensive function, 31
  expressions of, 17–18
  instrumental function, 30
  job related, 19
  nature of, 16–18
  order function, 32
  origins, 18
  value expressive function, 31–32
Aging and work, viii
American Association of Retired Persons,
  29
American Federation of State, County &
  Municipal Employees, 158
Assessment center, 114

B
Barfield, Richard, 148 n
Benefit policies, 150–63
Bettner, J., 151 n
Brainstorming, 174
Britt, Louis P. III, 10 n
Building an age-fair climate, 193
Buyout in retirement, 184

C
Career counseling, training for managers,
  100
Career information centers, 98
Career management, 82–106
  contingency plans, 104
  mid-life conflicts, 100–101
  multiple career paths, 98
  on-the-job development, 98
  period of decline, 101
  problems of older workers, 105
  second careers, 104
  self-analysis, 104
Career management process, 84
Career planning for scientific and technical
  personnel, 99
Career planning workshops, 98
Career stages, 101
Cascio, Wayne, 129 n
CBS, 158
Challenges to management, 11
Chase Manhattan Bank, 158
Clark, Merrell, 29
Climate, age-fair, 83

Confrontation, 170–77
Control Data Corporation, 94
Corporate strategic plans, 86

D
Delta Airlines, 94
Denning, K., 153
Doctors, S. I., 153
Doering, Mildred, 22 n
Dumping strategy, 185

E
Early retirement, 160–63
  cash bonus, 161–62
  extended health and life insurance, 162
  full pension benefits early, 162
  pension COLA, 162
  social security supplements, 161
Earnings penalty on Social Security, 9
Economic plight of elderly, 28
Economic pressures, 8
EEOC, 57
Elderly; *see* Older workers
Elimination strategy, 183
ERISA, 10
Estes, Carroll L., viii n
Evaluation avoidance, 59

F
Field, H. S., 116 n
Flexible retirement policies, 153–63
Flexible retirement policies in Sweden, 159
Fortas, Abe, 65 n
Functional age, 26

G
Generation gap, 164–67
Gerson, Herbert E., 10 n
Gordon, T. L., 174 n
Gray Panthers, 29
Greasing the skids, 185
Guidelines for change, 192
GULHEMP, 26

H
Hall, A., 148
Hall, Douglas T., 101
Harvard Business Review survey, 34–50
Health, capacities versus disabilities, 120–24
Health assessment, 123
Health evaluation guidelines, 123–24
Holley, W. H., 116 n
Human resource inventory, 91
Human resource management
  depreciation model, 129
  renewable asset model, 130–31
Human resource planning, 82–106
  Delphi method, 95

Human resource planning—*Cont.*
  effects
    of demographic trends, 92–93
    of economic trends, 93–94
    of legal trends, 94
    of occupational trends, 95
    of social value trends, 94–95
  model of process, 90
  progression charts, 97
  workforce analysis, 91

I

IBM, 94, 158
Inbasket exercise, in assessment center, 114
Individual retirement decision
  and social security, 148–49
  attitudinal factors, 146
  and career counseling, 149–50
  community factors, 146
  educational factors, 145
  family factors, 146
  financial factors, 145–46
  and flexible options, 153–63
  and government policies, 147–49
  health factors, 145
  and inflation, 148
  model of, 143
  occupational factors, 144
  and organizational norms, 152–53
  and organizational policies, 149–57
  and pensions and benefits, 150–63
  personal factors, 144–45
  race differences, 145
  sex differences, 145
  and social security, 148–49

J–K

Jerdee, Thomas H., 34 n, 119 n, 157 n
Job families, 98
Job posting, 98
Job redesign, 124
Johnson, Lyndon, 53
Johnson, T. R., 148 n
Kennedy, Edward M., 130
Koyl, Leon, 26, 27 n

L

Lazer, Harriet L., 153 n
Leaderless discussion group, in assessment center, 114
Legal pressures, 10
Likert, J. G., 174 n
Likert, R., 174 n
Lippman, W., 32
Long-term imperative, 12
Lunn, Robert O., 119 n, 120 n, 157 n

M

Maier, N. R. F., 174 n
Management development, 134–35
Management by objectives, 135
Mandatory retirement, 76–80, 183–84
  abolition of, 80
  arguments against, 76
  arguments favoring, 76
  benefit adjustments, 77
  effects of prohibition, 80
  excepted occupations, 77
Medical data, interpretation of, 120–24
Mentor-protege relationships, 177–80
Morale of older workers, 22
Morgan, James, 148 n

N

National Cash Register Company, 57
National Council on the Aging, viii, 29
National Older Workers Information System, 159
Neutral strategy, 186
Nussbaum, Bruce, 6, 7 n

O

Obsolescence
  combatting, 126–38
  costs, 128
  half-life, 128
  job, 127–38
  roots of, 129
Older workers
  accident proneness, 64
  cognitive functioning of, 26
  commitment of, 22–23
  confronting, 170–77
  day-to-day relationships, 164–80
  economic plight, 28
  health of, 25
  interest in learning, 29
  involvement, 22–23
  as mentors, 98
  morale, 22
  obsolescence, 126–38
  performance, 23–25
  physical decline, 26
  programs for, 159
  reassignment, 168–72
  retirement desires, 29
  sensory abilities, 26
  social involvement, 28–29
  values of, 166–67
Opinion survey, 46–48
Organizational will, 187

P

Paley, William, 158
Part time work, 137

Pension constraints, 49
Pension policy, 150–63
  cost of living increases, 162
  Sweden, 159
Pepper, Claude, 4, 33, 59
Performance appraisal, 108–24
  appeal mechanism, 116
  avoiding litigation, 115–16
  behavioral observation scales, 113
  behaviorally anchored rating scales, 113, 119
  central tendency effect, 115
  documentation, 116
  feedback, 115
  formats, 113
  halo effect, 115
  job analysis in, 112
  job descriptions in, 112
  job dimensions, 112
  leniency effect, 115
  management by objectives, 113, 119
  narrative, 113
  standards, 112
  training raters, 115
  trait scales, 113
Performance assessment, 108–24
  in combatting obsolescence, 131–32
Performance, confronting poor, 170–77
Performance review, 108–24
Peter Principle, 114
Phase-out, 122
Physical correlates of aging, 26
Policy implementation, 188
Policy statement on older employees, 187–88
Post-retirement
  employment, 137
  temporary employee pool, 137
Potential, assessment of, 114
Pre-retirement
  counseling, 102
  programs, 137
Pressures to promote women and minorities, 49
Problem solving process, 174
Proteges, 177–80

R
Reassignment, 168–72
Reduction in force, 88
Relationships, cross-generational, 164–80
Retention strategy, 186
Retirement counseling, 185
Retirement decision by employee, 142–63;
  see also Individual retirement decision
Retirement decision by management
  alternatives for low performers, 122

Retirement decision by management—
    Cont.
  alternatives for low performers—*Cont.*
    effects
      of age, 119–23
      of appraisal format, 119
      of health, 120–24
      of job requirements, 121
      of performance level, 119
      of personal circumstances, 117–18
      of race, 117–18
      of sex, 117–18
    and performance appraisal, 117
    union influence, 118
Retirement, flexible options, 122, 140–63
Retirement desires, 29
Rhodes, Susan, 22 n
Rosen, Benson, 34 n, 119 n, 157 n
Rosow, J. M., 150

S
Schneider, C. J., 152
Schuster, Michael, 22 n
Second career preparation, 137
Select Committee on Aging, 59
Senior employees; *see* Older workers
Sheppard, H. L., 30, 153
Shkop, Y., 153–54
Silver handshake, 29
Social involvement of elderly, 28–29
Social security, 148–49
Social security earnings penalty, 9
Standard Oil, 158
Status inconsistency, 167
Strategic planning, 86
Strategies, organizational, 182–90
Streib, G. F., 152
Super, Donald E., 101
Swenson, Carl, 30

T
Tax Equity & Fiscal Responsibility Act, 78
Technological change, 5–8, 85
Training and development, 132–38
  administrative employees, 135–36
  advisory council, 133
  coaching, 136
  corporate-wide programs, 136
  divisional centers, 136
  evaluation of, 137–38
  internships, 136
  on the job, 136
  job rotation, 136
  long range planning of, 138
  managerial, 134–35
  production employees, 135–36
  scientific and technical, 133–34

Training and development—*Cont.*
  survey of needs, 132
  tuition reimbursement, 137
Training expenditures in the United States, 137
Travelers Insurance Co., 158
Trends affecting older workers, 5–11
Tuition reimbursement, 137

U–V
Union Carbide Corporation, 98
United Auto Workers, 158

University of North Carolina Business Foundation, viii
Values, older versus younger workers, 166–67

W–Z
Walker, James W., 153 n
Weak law enforcement, 50
Work, changing nature of, 5–8
Zager, R., 150